SPAIN

SPAIN

Elli
Sept '89

Alma
sove, human being.

ILLUSTRATED BY CECILIA EALES

JAN MORRIS

BARRIE & JENKINS
LONDON

This edition first published in Great Britain in 1988 by
Barrie & Jenkins Ltd
289 Westbourne Grove, London W11 2QA

British Library Cataloguing in Publication Data

Morris, Jan, *1926 –*
Spain. — New illustrated ed.
1. Spain – Visitors' guides
I. Title
914.6′0483

ISBN 0 7126 2086 9

Typeset by SX Composing Ltd, Rayleigh, Essex
Colour separation by Reprocolor Llovet, Barcelona
Printed and bound by Printer Industria Grafica, Barcelona

CONTENTS

For
ELIZABETH,
again

AN INTRODUCTORY NOTE

This book portrays one of the most compelling of all countries at a turning-point in its history. In 1975 General Franco, for 35 years the dictator of Spain, died in his bed and left his country to begin afresh. Excluded for so long from the comity of Europe, clamped within the strait-jacket of despotism, Spain had become a country peculiarly on its own. Now it had a chance to re-enter the European mainstream, adapting itself to modern economic systems and becoming an economic partner with its peers.

My book is about that moment – about the Spaniards poised to rejoin the rest of us, but subject still to the mighty isolation of their past; but since such portentous historical moments recur throughout the history of Spain, perhaps it is about all Spanish moments, really.

TREFAN MORYS, 1988

Bay of Biscay

FRANCE

Coruña · Oviedo · Covadonga · Santander · San Sebastian
Asturias · Pasajes
Lugo · Bilbao · Guernica · Roncesvalles · Pyrenees
Santiago · Vizcaya · Pamplona
de Compostela · León · Montserrat
Galicia · Astorga · Burgos · Logroño · Corella · Alcalá del Ebro
Vigo · Duero River · Soria · Saragossa · Ebro River · Barcelona
Zamora · Tordesillas · Tarragona
Guadarrama Mountains
Duero River · Segovia · Alcalá de
Salamanca · Ávila · Madrid · Henares · Cuenca
Móstoles

S P A I N

PORTUGAL

Tague River · Aranjuez · Sagunto
Alcántara · Toledo · Valencia
Cáceres · New · La Mancha · Balearic
Guadiana River · Castille · Islands
Alenda · Palma
Badajoz · Alcoy
Jijona
Sierra Morena · Alicante
Guadalquivar River · Úbeda · Elche
Córdoba · Murcia
Huelva · Seville · Jaén · Andalucia · Cartagena
Priego de Córdoba
Granada · Almería · Mediterranean Sea
Ronda · Málaga · Trevelez
Atlantic Ocean · Cádiz · Fuengirola · Los Bolishes
Algeciras
Tarifa

AFRICA

N
W · E
S

PROLOGUE: THE GIST OF IT

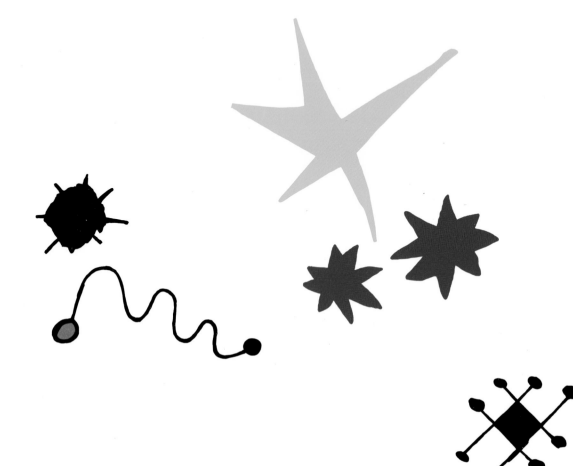

The centre of most Spanish cathedrals is dominated by the *coro*, a dark, carved, boxlike structure that blocks the grand prospect of the nave but provides an intellectual focus for the whole building. Here, beneath the glowing barrels of the organ pipes, the canons intone their litanies and the choirboys their harsh descants, the beadles shuffle past with messages or missals, the huge plain-chant hymnals stand open on their lecterns, and all the thought and reason of the cathedral seems to be concentrated. The *coro* is less like a sanctuary than a library, or perhaps the study of some misogynist theologian; and the visitor generally finds his way there first, to sniff its bookish atmosphere and inspect its choir stalls in the gloom, before he sets out to tour that mass of sculpture and sanctity, that museum of holy relics, sublime inventions, oddities, excesses, superstitions and splendours that is a Spanish church.

In the great cathedral that is Spain herself, the part of the *coro* is played by the palace-monastery called the Escorial, for there you may sense, stuffed darkly into granite labyrinths, all the forces that have shaped this tremendous and sometimes frightening country. It stands in the foothills of the Guadarrama mountains, with woods and snows behind its back, and the vast plateau of Castile stretching away to Madrid before it. It is rectangular, and enormous, and implacably severe, unrelieved by any softness of foliage or decoration: part a place of worship, part a royal palace, part a mausoleum, so big that it is officially classed as a city, with 86 staircases, 89 fountains, more than a thousand doors, 13 oratories, cells for 300 monks, tombs for 24 kings and queens, 16 patios, 2,673 windows, and a hundred miles of passages. Wide blank courtyards surround the walls of this marvel, a little town hangs respectfully about its purlieus, and from far away across the plain, even from the streets of Madrid herself, you can see it brooding there on the edge of the mountains, looking at once holy, menacing and obsessed.

The foothills of the Guadarrama Mountains

The Escorial was built by Philip II of Spain, grandson of Joan the Mad – whose chamber of insanity he once visited as a child, to find her crouched raving and in rags upon the floor, surrounded by plates of mouldering food. He began the building in 1563, to be his family tomb as well as his palace. He loved the raw austerity of the Castilian highlands, so pitilessly hot in summer, so bitter in the winter winds, and he was impelled by the fact that in his generation Spain had reached the apex of worldly power. She was the richest and most formidable nation on earth. From these rooms, Philip said, he 'ruled the world with two inches of paper', and he made the great building not only an expression of his own proud, suspicious character, but also a shrine of the values that were to govern Spain from his time into our own. Since Philip's day the history of this country has been generally melancholy and often tragic, but the style that was set in its golden age remains the ruling style today, and there is nothing out of date about the Escorial. In its conception, its flavour, even its meticulous Spanish workmanship, it might have been built yesterday: for only now, four centuries later, is Spain tentatively discarding the attitudes King Philip struck for her.

In these endless corridors and courtyards you may sense the Spanish taste for the grandiose and the overbearing, fostered in the false dawn of an imperial prime, and often vulgarized in bombast. In the coldness and bleakness of this building you may detect the aristocratic stoicism of Spain, something grandly ascetic in the character of the country, which often makes it feel otherworldly and aloof. In the inescapable presence of Philip himself, haunting every corner of his Escorial, you may fancy this nation's perennial yearning for a strong man at the centre, its recurrent instinct for autocracy. In the clear-cut pattern of the building, said to be grille-shaped in tribute to the martyrdom of St. Lawrence, you may see reflected the clarity and precision that characterizes so much of Spanish life. In its manner of command you may see how the centre of this large country has imposed its will upon the perimeter, stamping all with its own Castilian culture and keeping a watchful check on deviations. In the huge Basilica, embedded in the heart of the structure, you may realize how close the Christian faith has stood to the sources of authority in Spain. In the

The Escorial

ornate, cramped galleries of the royal tombs, with their spaces for monarchs yet to die, their separate vaults of bastards and in-laws, their neat little crests and chiselled pedigrees, their rotting-chamber where the corpse of the Queen-Regent Maria Christina, 'for political reasons', lies mouldering to this very day – in all this morbid splendour you may observe the Spanish love of hierarchy and formality, with its conviction that death is only a proper end to a familiar pattern.

Above all, in the pervading sadness of the Escorial, you may feel something of the tragedy of Spain, her lack of fulfilment. Here at the summit of the known world, Philip lived a dedicated and abstemious life, receiving the gorgeous ambassadors upon a throne of kitchen-chair simplicity, with a high brimless hat upon his head and his foot upon a gout-stool. His life was passed in work and prayer; his bedroom was a kind of cell; he was surrounded by the dossiers of State affairs, code keys and files of secret information. An aura of great power, fear, and sanctity invested him, so that the most experienced of the envoys entered his presence nervously, and even now there is something terrible about his memory. He died, however, miserably.

There he lay in ulcerous agony, a crowned skull on the table beside him, watching the rituals of the chapel through a spy-hole near his bed, ordering black cloth for his own mourning draperies, rehearsing the ritual of Extreme Unction, in such pain that he sometimes could not bear the weight of a sheet upon his body, in such gangrenous squalor, it is said, that his courtiers could not bring themselves to approach him. And when at last he died, to have ceaseless prayers for his soul said in the Basilica for two centuries to come – when he died in 1598, it was in the knowledge that already Spain's brief heyday was over, the vast empire was beginning to disperse, and two inches of Spanish paper, in the hands of a God-fearing Spanish aristocrat, had not been omnipotent after all.

All this you may sense in the Escorial still, and you may learn how the pride, resignation and disillusionment of Philip's Kingdom were to be projected into twentieth-century Spain. More than most countries, Spain feeds upon her own past. Even now her affairs are subject to the gloomy magnetism of the Escorial, or at least to the pole of emotions that this great work of faith and policy represents.

Spanish geographers are very fond of elevation graphs – diagrams which, by cutting an imaginary slice through the Iberian Peninsula, show how its altitudes vary from sea to sea. If you apply this technique to the slab of Spanish history, you will find that though the graph is often bumpy, its general outline is all too sadly simple. From the beginning of history to the sixteenth century, the Spaniards gradually climbed towards the pinnacle of their success – hindered often by wars and invasions, but steadily accumulating wealth, culture, prestige, and unity. From the sixteenth century until our times, on the other hand, they have been almost constantly slithering downhill, sometimes bravely digging their heels in, more often plunging helplessly downwards in a welter of despair and recrimination. Spanish history does not form a happy pattern, but at least it looks symmetrical.

The Spaniards have always been a warlike people, and the original Iberians were famous for their feats of arms. Some are remembered for drawing bulls in caves and others, the Beaker people, are thought to

13

have been the migrants who erected the stones of Stonehenge. But to the earliest chroniclers of their affairs, the Spaniards were above all soldiers – the original guerrillas. The early Phoenicians and the Greeks, who were merchants rather than conquerors, seem to have established their trading colonies in the peninsula without much trouble, but the Carthaginians and the Romans who followed them, with ambitions of dominion, were opposed by tribes-people of violent martial talent. It took two hundred years for the Romans to master Spain, and the country is littered with the legends of communities which, rather than submit to the legions, burnt their homes around them, or threw themselves *en masse* over precipices. It was the long resistance of the Spaniards that forced Rome to adopt conscription, and it was from a Spanish model that the Roman armourers copied the famous short sword of the legionaries. Spain was full of redoubtable peoples. The people of the centre cleaned their teeth in stale urine, the people of the north ate bear steaks and drank bulls' blood, the people of the north-west sacrificed their prisoners to read the omens in their entrails. 'Their bodies inured to abstinence and toil,' wrote one Roman observer in the first century before Christ, 'their minds composed against death, all practise a stern and constant moderation. They prefer war to ease, and should they lack foes without, seek them within.' The war-cry of the Asturians summed them up. It sounded like the howl of an insatiably ravenous wolf, and has been phoneticized thus: *Icucuuuu!*

But already the Spaniards, urine, bulls' blood, wolf-calls, and all, were clambering up that graph. From the Phoenicians they learnt to write, to use money, to mine for their metals. From the Greeks they learnt to grow vines and olives, and to make beautiful things. From the Romans they learnt so much that they eventually became the most advanced and cultivated of all the Empire's subject races. Spanish soldiers naturally became a mainstay of the legions, but during the six centuries of Roman occupation the Spaniards also matured marvellously in the gentler arts. Most of the later Roman literature came out of Spain, from the satires of Martial to the Stoic sermons of Seneca, and the emperors Trajan, Hadrian, Marcus Aurelius, and Theodosius the Great were all Spaniards. When the Romans withdrew at last, it was a prosperous Christian country that they left behind; and the Visigoths who succeeded them in the fifth century, driving out the rabble of miscellaneous barbarians that had swept in from Gaul, soon found themselves tempered by its culture, their crude, fissiparous Christianity smoothed into orthodox Catholicism, their rough manners softened and scented. From a cruel western land of dangerous peoples – the *ne plus ultra* of the ancient navigators, the *horrida et bellicosa provincia* of the Roman invaders – Spain had become a country to be coveted, civilized and productive, whose standards had declined indeed since the golden days of Rome, but whose prizes were well worth the plucking.

No wonder the Muslims, storming along North Africa in the fury of their seventh-century expansion, soon cherished designs upon the place. Only twenty miles of water separated Morocco from Spain, and in many ways the country seemed a kind of idealized Africa – Africa without the heat, without the drought, without the sand, the flies, or the diseases, where maidens 'as handsome as houris', so one Arab of the time thought, 'recline on soft couches in the sumptuous palaces of lords and princes'. In 711 the Muslims crossed the strait, egged on by dissidents on the other side. It took them only two years to subdue the whole of southern Spain, and most of the north too, and the last of the Visigothic kings, we are told, sank with such mystic finality into the marshes of

The Roman bridge
and the cathedral,
Córdoba

15

Cádiz that he was never seen again, only his horse with its golden trappings surviving mud-flecked to show the spot. The Moors, as the Spaniards called the mixed Arabs, Syrians, Egyptians, and Berbers of this conquest, made Spain the westernmost province of Islam, and stayed on her soil for seven hundred years.

Once again Spain profited. The Moors squabbled incessantly among themselves, but out of their tribal antipathies there presently evolved the supreme caliphate of Córdoba, which was set up in rivalry to the Abbasside dynasty of Baghdad, and was so cultured, sophisticated, broad-minded and fastidious a State that for a century southern Spain was the lodestar of Europe, and Córdoba herself was second in size only to Constantinople. Religion was free, in the great days of this admirable caliphate, women had equal educational chances, libraries, universities, and observatories flourished, poets abounded and musicians were great men. Life itself, which was seen elsewhere in Europe as a kind of probationary preparation for death, was interpreted as something glorious in itself, to be ennobled by learning and enlivened by every kind of pleasure. The Moors, springing out of an arid background, were the waterers of Spain, the gardeners: they brought a new grace to her culture, they taught her people the techniques of irrigation, and as their own spirit degenerated into excess and sybaritic fancy, so they infused into the Spanish stream some embryo traces of its romanticism – early inklings of swirl, smoulder, quarter-tone and castanet.

Granada

They never, however, quite obliterated Christian Spain. Even in the south there were Christian grandees who obtained for themselves a sort of autonomy, and in the drizzly north a little nucleus of Christians never surrendered at all. At the legendary battle of Covadonga in 718 a band of 31 Christians, we are told, halted the advance of 400,000 Muslims, and thus kept the Moors out of the mountains of Asturias; and around the memories of this feat, over the generations, there assembled the dream of reconquest. This was the age of the Cid and his fellow stalwarts of romance. Led by such magnificos, the Christians fought back in fits, starts, and marauds, gradually nibbling their way southwards again, sometimes fighting among themselves, sometimes cohering, sometimes turning coat to help a Muslim friend against a Christian enemy. It was a haphazard kind of Crusade, but by the end of the eleventh century the Christians, grouped in several principalities, had recaptured the central plateau of Spain. By the end of the thirteenth they had taken Córdoba, and mastered all but a southern coastal strip. And in 1492 the Catholic Monarchs of Christian Spain, Isabel of Castile and Ferdinand of Aragón, expelled the last of the Moorish kings from his delectable palace in Granada, and completed the liberation. The cross went up in the mosques of the Alhambra, somebody produced a grammar of the Castilian language, and Spain became recognizably herself.

Now we are approaching the top of that graph, for at this moment of her history Spain became, almost simultaneously, free, united, rich and powerful. She became free by the subjugation of the Moors. She became united because her two dominating Christian kingdoms, Castile and Aragón, were joined in marriage. She became rich and powerful because in the very month of the fall of Granada, when the last of the Moors tumbled out of the Alhambra to be forcibly baptized, Christopher Columbus was summoned to the presence of the Catholic Monarchs, and given a mandate to explore the western ocean. He discovered America, and instantly made Spain one of the Great Powers of the world. Now her indomitable adventurers, escaping from the impoverished gloom of her plateaus, strode irresistibly through Latin America, toppling the fantastic kingdoms of Aztec and Inca, building churches, missions, and palaces, sending home a dizzy stream of bullion. In the flush of excitement and achievement, the Spaniards seemed invincible. Charles I lopped the negative off the old tag, and adopted the slogan *plus ultra*, as if to imply that nothing was beyond the reach of Spain. The Pope grandly gave the Spaniards title to all land west of the Cape Verde Islands, and they themselves, by war and advantageous weddings, boldly extended their dominions until they ruled the greatest empire since the Romans.

The Hapsburg Charles I, father of Philip II, was Holy Roman Emperor too, and the territories he bequeathed to his son included the whole of South and Central America, much of what is now the United States, large chunks of France, the Low Countries, southern Italy, the Philippines, Ceylon, the Congo, and miscellaneous islands and settlements from Sumatra to the Azores. When Philip moved into the Escorial, having supervised every finicky detail of its still unfinished construction, Spain had reached the top. She was the supreme Power, and the universal champion of Catholicism. Her culture a rich mixture of Christian and Moorish, Iberian and Roman, her national image so proud that the Spanish patrician was Europe's cynosure of elegance and command, her voyagers outrageously swashbuckling and her experience of the New World unrivalled, she must have seemed, in the eyes of less vivid States, a very prodigy of a nation. She was flamboyantly, aggressively Christian, and God seemed to be distinctly on her side. Truth, the Spaniards thought, was not only indivisible, but essentially Spanish: and if an empire knows the only truth, who can supersede it?

But every empire thinks it knows, and the Spaniards did not stay long upon that glittering apex. Gangrene and exhaustion set in, upon the nation as upon the king, and when Philip's catafalque was borne away, and his body committed to the *pudridero* in the vault, Spain had already set out upon the long descent. Everything, excepting only art, rotted. At home and abroad enemies were recklessly made in the cause of Catholic unity. The treasures of the New World were squandered in war and political mayhem all over Europe. The Dutch rebelled, and the Catalans, and the Protestant English, who had already defeated the

Armada, now went about crowing heretical triumph. The glory turned out to be no more than a mirage, and even the heroic past of Spain went sour, as Cervantes mocked its pretensions of chivalry in the book that is said to have killed a nation. Spain was rich in talents still, in painters and writers, mystics and philosophers, but behind her façade of pomp she was already a kingdom of poor men and self-delusions. The sap of the Moor had dried, as the irrigation works were allowed to crumble. The old centrifugal forces of Spain, inherited from tribe and rival kingdom, revived to plague the body politic, and tug at the strong nub of power that was represented by the Escorial. Never was a nation's moment of supremacy quite so brief, or quite so dazzling; and never again was Spain to be quite certain about her role in the world.

In 1700 the Hapsburgs were succeeded upon the throne of Spain by the Bourbons, a family whose name has become synonymous with decay, and under their aegis the nation sank into provincial impotence. The War of the Spanish Succession stripped the Spaniards of their European empire, plus their own Rock of Gibraltar. The Napoleonic Wars led first to the loss of Louisiana and Trinidad, then to the calamity of Trafalgar, and finally to the French occupation of the peninsula and the elevation of Joseph Bonaparte to be King of Spain. The Peninsula War – which the Spaniards call the War of Independence – restored the Bourbons to power and demonstrated the ferocious fighting spirit of the Spanish working people, but it only emphasized Spain's dependence upon more powerful

A view of Gibraltar from the mainland

19

allies. A succession of colonial wars led only to the independence of the South American republics. The two Carlist Wars, concerned with succession to the throne, ravaged the Spanish countryside and inflamed the people in internecine passion. The Rif wars in North Africa drained Spain's coffers and decimated her man-power. The Spanish-American War, ending ignominiously in 1898, not only lost her Cuba, the last of her great colonies, but also demonstrated her isolation in the world, neither fish nor fowl among the States, proud but poor, famous but powerless, imperial without an empire. At home there were constant conflicts between traditionalists and liberals, landowners and working classes, centralists and federalists, and for thirty years of the Victorian era the titular ruler of Spain was the nymphomaniac Isabel II, whose red-plush love-nest above a restaurant in Madrid is still shown to tourists of scholarly instinct. Even the Industrial Revolution failed to ignite. Even the artistic genius dried up. Never was a century more disastrous to a nation than the nineteenth century was to Spain.

So she limped into our own times – with one half of her being, for the other half was still lingering wistfully with the Cid and the conquistadores. She was a mess of a country: addled by bitter politics at home – between 1814 and 1923 there were forty-three *coups d'état;* embroiled in constant wars in the pathetic remnants of her empire, now confined to a few sandy or fetid enclaves in Africa; diplomatically a cipher, strategically so inessential that the First World War contemptuously passed her by. Conflicting ideologies tortured her – dogmas of monarchy, theocracy, despotism, democracy, socialism, anarchism, Communism. Her rural poverty and urban squalor periodically erupted into violence. Her colonial policies were so inept that in 1921 her Moroccan army was annihilated in the Rif. A dictator, Primo de Rivera, came and went; in 1931 the last of the Bourbons, bowing himself out of the chaos, gave way to a left-wing Republic; and in 1936 all these centuries of failure, schism, and frustration gave birth to that ultimate despair, the Spanish Civil War.

It was theoretically a revolt by the Nationalist conservatives against the Republic, but in the end it was really a double revolution – by Right and Left against Centre. The passions it brought so hideously to the boil had been simmering for five centuries, and were so wounding

Street scene with graffiti, El Puerto de Santa Maria

that to this day the scars still show. '*The Others*' is how Spaniards of the defeated Left sometimes referred to their adversaries, and this dark reticence, so muffled, so oblique, properly expressed the heritage of the conflict. For more than forty years after General Francisco Franco's victorious Nationalists set up their autarchy of the Right, Spain was trapped within the aftermath of war, subjected to a despotism whose first aim was to ensure that the *status quo* would never be broken again. Only with Franco's death in 1975, and the re-establishment of the monarchy as he decreed, did Spain begin to escape from her crippling inhibitions.

What next? We do not know. Here the graph peters out, with King Juan Carlos on the throne of Spain and a liberal democracy spluttering and sometimes exploding into life around him, complete with all the paraphernalia of parties, elections, strikes, protests and graffiti. Spain is a democracy now, but still the Spanish role remains uncertain, the Spanish destiny seems unfulfilled, and we can only look at the

Spanish future through a veil of memory and conjecture – 'a cloud of dust,' as the philosopher José Ortega y Gasset once put it, 'left in the air when a great people went galloping down the highroad of history'.

Generally the visitor, adjusting his eyesight to the shadows, pauses for a time in the *coro* to consult his guidebook – resting his back against a sculpted crocodile, perhaps, or propping the book upon a fourteenth-century music-stand. When he feels he has the gist of the building, has mastered its origins and sorted out its periods, he sets off to explore the rest of it: and so the traveller too, if he has read the text of the Escorial, may feel equipped to inspect the aisles and chapels of Spain, where the dust loiters and dances on the sun-shafts, and you can faintly hear the rumble of the cars outside.

1
ISLE
BARATARIA

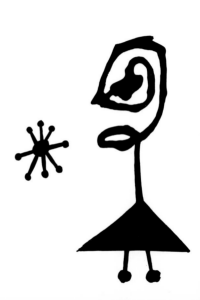

Spain is almost an island – a fragment crudely soldered, so the poet Auden thought, to the shape of Europe. Whichever way you enter her, from Portugal, France, Gibraltar, or the open sea, instantly you feel a sense of separateness – a geographical fact exaggerated by historical circumstance. The first of the invading Moors actually thought Spain was an island, and it was the Phoenicians, already sensing this seclusion or withdrawal, who called the country *Spania* – a word which some dullard philologists believe to mean The Land of Rabbits, but which all proper amateurs of Spain accept in its alternative interpretation, The Hidden Land.

The best entrance of all is the pass of Roncesvalles, the most heroic of the ten defiles that pierce the Pyrenees. It is a high, demanding route, resonant with romance. Here, a thousand years ago, the knight-errant Roland blew his enchanted horn so deafeningly that the birds fell dead about him, and here the savage Basques, hurling themselves upon Charlemagne's rear-guard, slaughtered half his men-at-arms. Through the pass of Roncesvalles, throughout the Middle Ages, caravans of pilgrims plodded southwards to the shrine of St. James at Santiago de Compostela, carrying forests of palm-crosses and singing brave hymns. Potentates of every era have passed this way into Spain, spies and ambassadors, merchants and marriage brokers, princesses destined for

A landscape in the Pyrenees

24

A village in the Pyrenees

Spanish thrones and holy men on their way to sainthood. Here Marshal Soult fought a running battle with the British, as they chased the French out of the peninsula in 1813, and along this road thousands of wretched refugees stumbled into France during the Spanish Civil War. Roncesvalles is one of the classic passes of Europe, and a properly sombre gateway into Spain.

Winter is the time to make the journey. Then, as you approach the pass, the Pyrenean ramparts of Spain are at their most suggestive: brown, purple, and forbidding, with blushes of pink along their high snow-ridges, and wild white clouds eddying down their valleys. Beyond them, you feel, floodlights are perpetually blazing upon the stage of Spain, and you approach them with all the excitement of a visit to the theatre. There is a fanfare to the very name of Spain, and no nation offers an image more vivid. She seems to follow no fashion, obey no norm. She has generally stood aloof from the events of the recent past, from the Second World War to the nuclear race, and while to some her allure is only the spell of bathing beach and cheap wine, to others she stands apart because she does not yet feel reconciled to the twentieth century – has not quite succumbed to those pressures of materialism which we, like so many dim Frankensteins, half regret having devised.

Spain is one of the absolutes. Most States nowadays are willy-nilly passive, subject always to successive alien forces. Spain still declines in the active mood. She is not a Great Power, but in her minor way she is one of the prime movers still – still a nation that sets its own standards. To us poor ciphers of the computer culture, us cosmopolitan, humanist, cynical serfs of the machine, nothing is more compelling than the

Real Colegiata, Roncesvalles

drama, at once dark and dazzling, of that theatre over the hills – the vast splendour of the Spanish land-scape, the intensity of Spain's pride and misery, the adventurous glory of a history that set its seal upon half the world, the sadness of a decline that edged so inexorably from triumph to tragedy, through so many centuries of rot. All this, distilled in blazing heat and veno-mous cold, dusted by the sand of Africa, guarded by that mountain barricade above you – all this seems to await your arrival, beyond the pass of Roncesvalles.

Presently it all comes true. Skidding upwards through the windy sleet, soon you reach the head of the pass, and stand at the gate of Spain. All is deserted and forlorn up there. An old snow-plough lies tilted beside the road, a line of army huts lies derelict among the firs. Be-tween the trees there broods the gaunt Augustinian monastery of Ron-cesvalles, with roofs that look like corrugated iron, and a great wet empty courtyard. A woman looks out of a door as you pass through its sullen hamlet. Two hooded policemen, huddled against the wind, re-spond numbly to your wave. Your first moments of Spain, if theatrical enough, hardly make you tingle.

But then you turn a corner out of the woodland, and suddenly there before you, below the level of the mist, there unfolds the great plain of the Ebro, with the foothills sweeping down towards the river. Space immeasurable seems to lie down there. All is brown but magnificent monotony – monotony of the desert kind, that has something mystic and exciting to it. In the middle distance a group of gypsies hastens with caravans, donkeys, and skinny dogs along the road, and beyond them all Spain seems to be expecting you – Spain of the shrines, Spain of the knights-errant, Spain of the guitars, the bull-rings, and the troglodytes. That evening you will sleep in Pamplona, where they let the young bulls loose in the streets on the feast of St. Fermín, where legend says they once killed ten thousand Jews to celebrate a prince's wedding, where the church bells sound like the clashing of coal shovels in the small hours, and the hotel pillows feel as though they are stuffed with mule-hair.

It is partly environment that gives you this feeling – the feeling that you have burst into some bizarre private world beyond the mountains. The land of Spain resembles no other, so four-square and rough-hewn is its out-line (the shape of an open bull-hide, so the old geographers thought). It is like an immense fortress. Its aver-age height is about two thou-sand feet, and mountains rise almost sheer from its coasts, leaving only narrow seaside strips or estuaries.

Within these mountain walls a vast plateau extends, like the bailey of a castle – once thickly forested, now stripped of its topsoil, and itself so corrugated by mountain ranges that wher-ever you are in Spain, at any time of the year, you are never sur-prised to see the distant blur of the snow summits. This is a harsh high-land country, second only to Swit-zerland, among the nations of Europe, in its general altitude. The

Young bulls in the streets of Pamplona

27

highest road in Europe is in Spain, above the city of Granada. The highest inhabited village is said to be Trevélez, in the Alpujarra mountains of the south. Perpetual wind is one of the characteristics of Spain, the lowering *levante* of the east, the Atlantic bluster of the south-west, and above all the dagger wind that scours the central *meseta* – a wind, so the proverb says, that can kill a man, but can't blow out a candle. It is a climate of ferocious extremes: when I picked up a Spanish newspaper one morning at the end of May, I found that on the previous day the temperature at Córdoba had been thirty-two degrees centigrade, while the temperature at León had been *four*.

Few dependable rivers soften this cruel terrain. Except in the north-west, Spanish rainfall is sparse and erratic – in Alicante in 1882 more rain fell in one day than fell in all the rest of the year put together. When it does rain, or the mountain snows melt, then the rivers flood ferociously down to the sea, often destroying roads and bridges, and carrying away good soil; but for most of the time they are dry, and are frequently used as mule-tracks themselves, so that a cool blue tracery on the map turns out to be only a hot pebbly strip of wasteland, with goats nibbling at its scrubby grass, and a limp horse or two breathing heavily in the shade of its bridges. There are only five big rivers in Spain – the Ebro, the Guadalquivir, the Guadiana, the Tagus and the Duero – spread across the country like the open fingers of a man's hand. For the rest, some of

In the Alpujarra Mountains

the oldest Spanish jokes concern their lack of water. The River Manzanares at Madrid, one of the most anaemic of them all, was once described as looking like 'a university town in the long vacation'. Somebody else said that if you wanted to see it, you should jump into a bus the moment it rained, or the river would be gone before you got there. Philip II, who threw the great Puente de Segovia across its stingy stream, was told by a candid critic that he either ought to sell the bridge or buy himself a new river. Water is one of the prime preoccupations of Spanish life. The pump is the traditional village focus, and until very recently the sale of contract of every Madrid apartment specified where the water came from. The most absolute demarcation lines in Spain are the lines that separate the dry land from the damp, the arid from the humid zones, the desert from the irrigated plain – the purgatory, in short, from the paradise.

For the Spaniards live in clusters, like squatters around the waterholes. Only in the green regions of the north can they live like other countrymen of the West, comfortably among their own fields. Elsewhere in Spain they are crowded always beside the water – in big river cities, in minuscule wellhead hamlets, or in the rich irrigated valleys that the Moors first made. Wide empty areas separate one pocket of habitation from another, and they themselves range in fecundity from the luxuriant to the lunar. The people of the Valencian littoral inhabit the most fertile slab of land in Europe, and the most densely populated agricultural region outside Egypt and India: its oranges sometimes weigh seven pounds apiece, and its markets seem to burst with plump, rosy, earthy, sweet-smelling nutriment. The people of the Murcian coast, on the other hand, inhabit the fringe of a desert – one of the most barren and depressing of them all, its surface all scrubby scree, its rocks streaked with sulphurous colours, its valleys permanently waterless. The average wheat yield in Logroño, in the north, is nearly six times as great as the average yield in Almería, in the southeast. The coastline around Málaga, in the south, is as lush as any tropical shore,

The River Iregua, Logroño

29

with its sugar-canes and its thick sweet wines. The plateau of the interior, where the villages often look more like piles of rubble than human habitations, can be as dismal and demanding as any *altiplano* of Peru. The mountain country of Asturias, whose hearty hillmen drink draught cider and eat smoked trout, offers the same kind of rude sufficiency as do the Highlands of Scotland.

And yet, such is the power of the Spanish presence, all is unmistakably one country – the desperately dry, the obscenely fertile, the rough green mountain country. Whether the tree is a palm or a northern pine, the wind that sways it could only be Spanish, and the earth beneath it smells of Spain.

Partly it is plain old-fashionedness that makes Spain feel so special. She has a fatal weakness for the past. When the French were building in the Gothic style, she was still building Romanesque. When they moved into the Renaissance, she was still building Gothic. She retained her mediaeval values when they had long been abandoned elsewhere in Europe, so that at Spanish universities in the eighteenth century they were still wondering whether Copernicus was right, and anxiously debating whether the sky was made of metal or of fluid. No Beethoven symphony was performed in Madrid until 1866. It was only in the present century that the most primitive of the Spaniards, in the shuttered valleys near Salamanca, first heard of God. When Mr. Gerald Brenan went to live in Andalusia after the First World War, his neighbours assumed that he had been fighting the Moors, and were of the firm opinion that Protestants were people with tails.

This time-lag still makes Spain an anachronism among the nations. Her industrial revolution is really only happening now, and in many ways she retains the simplicity, even the innocence, of a pastoral nation. A Victorian propriety and formality, too, makes the stranger feel that his passage through the mountains has been a return in time. Carriages still sway down Andalusian lanes, with ladies chatting in their cushioned recesses, and coachmen flicking stray dogs with long leather whips. Hay carts still rumble down the hill lanes of Galicia, the bullocks sweating in the shafts and the yokels in straw hats hanging on

The banks of the River Ouero, Zamora

behind. Splendid brass-bound loco-
motives snort in steam and metal
polish down Spanish railways.
Spanish country buses, so
bumpy and gregarious, still
flaunt the rollicking gusto of
the mail coaches. Except in
the sophisticated cities,
Spanish courtships are
still discreet, Spanish
mothers are still domi-
nant, Spanish men are
very manly and Spanish
women usually chaste.
Spanish towns stand so
far apart from one
another that they often
still feel like City-States,
wrapped up in their own
parochial affairs, looking
inwards to the cathedral
and the coffee shop
rather than outwards to
the rockets or the situation in the Middle East.

Nothing indeed could feel much more proper and permanent than
life in such a Spanish country city – *La Capital* to the peasants of the
surrounding countryside, but to the foreigner no more than a middle-
sized market town on the way to somewhere else. Life has changed
beyond description, I am told, since the early thirties, when a young
man hardly dared speak to an unmarried girl, and courtship was conducted under restrictions not merely puritanical, but actually Islamic.
It has changed enormously, once again, since the 1960s. Even so, to an
outsider life in a Murcia, a Zamora, or a Jaén seems marvellously
unruffled by social progress.

In the market, for instance, the homely ways of the countryside are
still reassuringly lively – the butcher skins a sheep before your eyes as

easily as peeling an apple, the hens are tied together with hairy string upon their basket-tops, there is chicken-earth upon the egg-shells, and the market woman wraps up your radishes in thick brown paper. In the shopping streets the bourgeoisie parades past the cafés in a dazzle of polished shoes and spotless gloves, its small moustaches carefully clipped, its hair impeccably curled, its infants primped and frilly. Outside the cathedral knots of busy priests are engaged in earnest conversation, standing very close to each other, and talking with such intensity that sometimes the brims of their wide hats actually touch, and knock the whole argument askew. Along the river promenade elegant pigtailed schoolgirls saunter home, swinging their satchels, and an old mendicant sits on a wall selling a knobbly assortment of herbs. There are big pink jars in the shelves of the apothecaries, and huge wine-stained barrels on the wineshop floors, and scrumptious sticky cakes in the cakeshops, and the liqueur bottles in the cafés are decorated with the gold medals of forgotten exhibitions and the escutcheons of extinct dukes. Among the flower-beds of the plaza the starched nannies gossip in a Watteau-like tableau of prams, aprons, sailor suits, and eagerly eavesdropping little girls; from the huge dim-lit windows of the Casino (as they call a club in Spain) four or five apparently mummified figures glare glassily at the passers-by, with tumblers of what looks like lukewarm water listlessly at their elbows.

And in the evening, when the *paseo* begins in the main square when the young men stroll purposefully up and down in one direction, and the girls giggle in groups in the other, when the municipal officials emerge pomaded from their departments and the young officers of the garrison, smoothing their glove-fingers, clamber out of their taxis and stride gallantly into the crowd – when the evening *paseo* begins, with all its unwritten formalities of flirtation and politesse, then you may feel yourself back in some long-dead Europe, the England of Barchester and the Proudies, perhaps, or Gogol's vanished Russia. The dignitaries grow grander as the evening wears on; and the subalterns will stay talking indefinitely at the salute, unless you implore them, my dear fellows, not to stand upon formality.

It is very charming to see, but sometimes the nostalgia of Spain has a more elemental quality: when an ore train plods across an endless landscape for example, with a plume of its black smoke in the evening light, and a long clanking snake of wagons across the tableland; or in some hangdog mining town, Dickensian in filth and gloom, where the old women grub for waste coal among the railway sidings, and make you think of Poor Susan; or in the Hogarthian slums of Barcelona, where the sailors' brothels are, the prostitutes are busted like pouter pigeons. The archaism of Spain is often touching, but often tough. The Spanish folk costumes have almost disappeared, surviving only in a kerchief here, a coloured apron there, or the clodhopping clogs of the north-west; but the peasantry of Spain is still marvellously earthy, and the miners of the north are dauntingly militant. This is still a frugal, sober, strong people, rich in men of the yeoman kind – lorry drivers, petty officers, mechanics, head porters, farm workers you would trust not only with your hay-making but with your life or your daughter too. *Hombre!* is the Spanish countryman's habitual greeting – *Man!* – and such straight, square old courtesies reflect what is best about the old-fashionedness of Spain: something frank and comradely, unaffected by time or money, rooted in the conviction that a man's a man for a' that. Part of the Spaniard's strength lies in his stubborn regard for the past.

In most languages of the West we use the same form of farewell – Goodbye, *Adieu, Addio, Adios*! Only in Spain, though, will you occasionally hear some fine old countryman, with a handshake like mahogany, spell it out in three grave separate words: *Go with God!*

33

Barcelona, the port

Spain is distinct, furthermore, because she has style. In a prosaic age she is not afraid to be patrician. She has always had the grand manner – 'the arrogant and insolent grace', as a French historian once described it – and sometimes even the *noblesse oblige*: one of the most Spanish of all pictures is Velázquez's wonderful *Surrender of Breda*, nicknamed *The Lances*, in which the superb Marquis de los Balbases receives the sword of his defeated Dutch adversary with a smile of ineffably considerate regret. Spain is a high-flown country. Marquises, dukes, and counts abound, and the traditions of Spain are rich with the conduct normally expected of nobles. Alonso de Guzmán, a thirteenth-century Spanish hero, allowed the Moors to kill his own son beneath the walls of Tarifa rather than surrender the town to them – he threw down his own dagger for the execution, crying, 'Kill the boy! I'd rather lose six sons than surrender!' Seven hundred years later Colonel Ituarte Moscardó, defending the Alcazar at Toledo for General Franco, allowed the enemy to kill his son too, rather than give up the fortress – 'Commend your soul to God,' he told the boy over the telephone, 'shout *Viva España*, and die like a hero!' Spain loves such postures, at once tragic and defiant, just as she has a persistent regard for flags, tall horses, and splendid isolation.

And often enough even those innumerable Spaniards who reject such values, who profess themselves internationalists, egalitarians, or modern materialists, nevertheless often possess an embarrassingly patrician style themselves. Most Spaniards are, to use an unfashionable term for a fast-vanishing condition, gentlemen. They are, rich or poor, angry or complacent, to the manner born. Nobody will treat the stranger with more elegant ease than the raggety peasant of Aragón or Castile, with his old cloak slung about his shoulders, his bruised hat on his head, his chin a little prickly and his hand calloused by a lifetime's labour: he will turn on his donkey as though sitting in the saddle of some magnificent thoroughbred, he will look you straight, solemn, and courteous in the eye, and he will answer your inquiry in a Spanish so distinguished and precise that it might be an extract from some recorded language course. He always makes you feel welcome, he never patronizes you, he always knows when to go, and he does not gush.

The Spanish castes are indeed distinct, though hard for the stranger to distinguish because there are no class accents. When great issues are at stake, hatred between them can be cruelly inflamed. Of the fourteen thousand regular officers in the Spanish Army at the beginning of the Civil War, only two hundred chose to fight for the Left: of the eight thousand regular non-commissioned officers, not more than a score chose to fight for the Right. It is apparently not envy, however, that excites these passions – the Spanish revolutionary does not usually covet riches for himself. In normal times Spaniards of all classes treat each other with a casual courtesy, almost a familiarity, that suggests to me the oddly easy relationship between master and serf in Tsarist Russia. Spanish Catholicism partly accounts for this lack of awkwardness, with its emphasis on Death as the great leveller, and some say too that it is an echo of the Roman's family attitude towards his slave. Whatever its origins, one reason for the success of the old Spanish armies is said to have been their democratic ease of intercourse, officers and men sharing the same mess; and if you ever visit one of the great fairs of Andalusia, when the landowning families come to town with their splendid horses and their flouncy polka-dots – if ever you mingle with the Andalusian gentry at such a festivity, you will find that grandees, belles, grooms, lackeys and all seem to converse with a dashing kind of fellowship, so that you are hard put to tell which is master, which is man and sometimes (for they are a lean and handsome lot) even which is horse.

It is this independence of manner, this head-high and straight-eyed ambience, that makes Spain feel so awfully noble, and keeps its *aficionados* dewy-eyed with thoughts of uprightness and individuality. In these austere and desolate landscapes there is indeed something bravely perpendicular about a man, something that makes him feel a finer, or at least an intenser, species than he is elsewhere. One powerful reason for the separateness of Spain is the fact that she always feels *more so*. In this country everything seems to be heightened, as by some elevating drug, and people in particular seem crueller, stubborner, kinder, and always grander. Spanish philosophical conceptions are full of synonyms for this loftiness of spirit, and slushy devotees of the culture are only too anxious to translate them – *alma*, for instance, which means more than merely soul, but is something almost anatomically detectable, or *casticismo*, which is more than just purism, but has come to stand for the very quality of Spanishness, the elusive but always pungent substance that floats around you the moment you cross the Spanish frontier.

And this exalting influence of Spain is catching, and makes the visitor, too, feel his *alma* swelling, rather like the mumps. Nothing expresses the mescalin quality of this country better than the bull-fight, that lurid and often tawdry gladiatorial ritual, which generally repels the northerner in the theory, but often makes his blood race in the act. All kinds of unexpected instincts are revived by this Spanish spectacle. The trumpet sounds; the gate falls open; the bull storms stocky, puzzled, and fuming into the arena; instantly the foreigner, overwhelmed by the glare, the colour, the mass emotion, the pageantry, and the heat of the moment, feels himself to be in some barbaric dissecting room, where all that is worst about Man is exposed to heartless floodlights. It is not at all a pleasant spectacle – not a sport at all. Blood runs, men are often wounded, poor padded blindfold horses are gored, the bull inevitably dies and is dragged out for beef. The crowd all around, that Greek chorus of the bull-ring, with its little cigars clenched between its teeth, its cardboard sun-visors on its foreheads, its one-peseta cushions plumped beneath its bottoms on the hard seats – the crowd all around seems animated, to the foreign eye, chiefly by a brutish lust for blood. 'I would not have been

A bullfight

37

displeased,' wrote Nelson to his wife after watching a bull-fight, 'to have seen the spectators tossed.'

And yet, such is the contagion of Spain, if you sit it out for long enough you will probably succumb yourself to the savage magic of the *corrida*. As its ghastly parade continues, circus tinsel beside high tragedy, as death succeeds death and blood blood, as the young gods are cheered around the arena or hissed out of sight, as the silent old horses topple in and the tossing caparisoned mules drag the carcases out — as the band thumps away at its music and the evening shadow creeps across the ring, so you will feel yourself, hour by hour, fight by fight, half united with the fierce multitude at your side. The nobility of death, so the experts assure us, is the point of the bull-fight — the ultimate Moment of Truth that comes, in the end, to us all; and before very long you too may feel that, through the blood lust and the intolerance, something of grandeur emerges. If you are unlucky, your *corrida* will be one long inept butchery, odious to watch; but if you have chosen well you may see a kill by one of the masters, short, calm, elegant, almost sacerdotal. The beast, after one clean, almost imperceptible sword-thrust, sinks slowly to its knees. The matador, as proud and kind as any victorious Marquis, reaches out a gentle hand, in a movement infinitely graceful and brotherly, to touch his dying adversary between the horns. It is a sentimental moment perhaps, possibly deceitful, certainly theatrical; but as that garlic crowd greets the gesture with a long deep sigh of admiration, so you may respond yourself to some inner *pasodoble*, and feel the old Spaniard stir in you.

All this adds up to the specialness of Spain, but in some ways it is illusory. If you drive down to the Ebro from Pamplona, and turn eastward along the river, presently you will reach the island that Sancho Panza governed. It is not an island at all, as any local will hasten to tell you; but it is the original, so tradition tells us, of the Isle Barataria, which Sancho ruled with such sturdy success through nine chapters of *Don Quixote*. Here occurred the ultimate illusion of that hallucinatory masterpiece. Here Sancho himself was deluded. He soon saw through the specious allure of power (though he 'ordained so many good things that to this day they are preserved in that place and called the Constitution of the Great Sancho Panza'); but he really did suppose that the territory assigned to him was an island – down the foothills of the Pyrenees, beside the Saragossa railway line.

Nowhere in western Europe could be much more dismal than the Isle Barataria today, reverted once again into a hamlet called Alcalá del Ebro, and slumped upon a bend of the river in an attitude of awful dejection. Its houses are mostly mean, its narrow streets are sloshed with winter mud or choked with dust, its river is brown and sluggish, and all day long there clank and clatter past the village, slung in containers from an overhead conveyor, loads of salt-rock destined for a factory beside the level crossing. It was called Barataria, Cervantes says, either because that was its name anyway, or because of its exceedingly low real-estate value – *baratura* means cheapness. I incline to the latter interpretation, for it seems to me a dominion with no asset but its Spanishness. It lives by *casticismo* – its courtesy, its arid landscape all about, the mud in its streets, the solemn faces at its saloon door. There is nothing special about the place, except its famous fable and its poverty; but in such a village, with such an association, you can appreciate how insular is the pride of Spain, and how delusory.

There is no country in Europe more introspective than Spain, and few admire themselves more. It is true that the Spaniard is subject to fits of wild self-criticism – 'We are a backward nation, we lack culture, we are not formal enough, we can never catch up, never

Alcalá del Ebro

39

trust a Spaniard.' More often, though, he still seems convinced, for all the ignominious evidence of the centuries, that his nation is not only best, but also altogether unique. Even in Strabo's time the Spaniards used to boast that they had been a literary and law-abiding nation for more than six thousand years (though since the Spanish year then lasted four months, the brag was less majestic than it sounds). On every Spanish passport, the historian Angel Ganivet once said, there were written the invisible words: 'This Spaniard is authorized to do whatever he wants.' In Spain foreigners have generally been regarded as inferiors, and the Fleming courtiers who came to Spain with the Hapsburgs were so generally despised that their very name, some people think, entered the language in derogation – *flamenco*, which now means a kind of song and dance, apparently used to mean an oafish vagabond. If you ask a Spaniard who fought the Battle of Trafalgar, he will tell you the Spanish and the British, quite forgetting the French; if you ask him who fought the Peninsular War, he will say the Spanish and the French, quite forgetting the British. Spaniards prefer not to be laughed at, and do not much like losing: they tend to remember only what is flattering to Spain, and they readily believe the State schoolmaster, when he says there is no nation on earth so famous, so successful, so rich, or so powerful as theirs.

Thus the genius of Spain is of an exceptionally private kind. Considering the age, activity, and ability of this nation, it is surprising how few Spaniards are generally known to the world today: among monarchs, only Isabel, Ferdinand, Philip II; among fighting men only Cortés and Pizarro; among writers, Cervantes, Lope de Vega, Galdós, Federico García Lorca; among thinkers, St. Ignatius, St. Theresa, St. John of the Cross, Miguel de Unamuno and Ortega y Gasset;

Daroca, Saragossa
Goya's birthplace

40

The windmills of La Mancha

among composers, Vitoria and Falla; among painters, El Greco, Zurbarán, Murillo, Velázquez, Goya, Picasso, Dali, Miró; among scientists, the inventor of the autogyro; among statesmen, General Franco. It is not many, for such a nation, and the reason perhaps is that Spaniards create essentially for Spaniards. *Don Quixote*, though it obviously has its universal meanings, is essentially a book about Spain – not a vision of the world, like Shakespeare's plays; and the Spanish language itself, though a hundred million speak it every day, is often more a barrier than a bridge. Sometimes the Spaniard will resent your attempts to use it. Sometimes he believes it to be physically impossible for an alien to understand it. Sometimes he cannot convince himself that you are actually speaking it, and sometimes, like an Edwardian Englishman, he is of the opinion that if you don't understand what he himself is saying in it, then you ought to, especially when he's talking so loud.

It is not offensive, this kind of chauvinism, only assertive – and sometimes sad. Older Spaniards are often pathetically ignorant of the world outside, and its intrusion can pitiably shake their equanimity. Even the most gaily soigné of citizens, if you plump him in a salon full of foreigners, often looks strangely self-conscious and ill-at-ease, like a man in a dress shop, and it is astonishing how few Spaniards even in

Madrid, the capital, speak a single word of any language but their own. The feeblest cooking in Europe is the Spanish, when it swops its fine old stews, crabs and partridges for some dismal approximation of the French cuisine. As for the cities of Spain, they only begin to feel provincial when they abandon their ancient isolated hauteur, and try for cosmopolitanism.

Spain is always conscious of her own symbolisms, and rightly so. 'Spain *hurts* me,' cried the essayist Miguel de Unamuno fifty years ago. 'When I speak of Spain,' wrote the poet Antonio Machado in the thirties, 'I speak of Man.' Time and again Spain has been a cockpit, where the conflicts of the world have had their first round, and sometimes even their last. It was by the Treaty of Tordesillas, still a very grand little Castilian

Street scene in Madrid

town, that the Borgia Pope Alexander VI partitioned the New World between Spain and Portugal – 'All Lands Discovered or Hereafter to Be Discovered in the West, towards the Indies or the Ocean Seas'. It was the Synod held at Elvira, near Granada, some time in the fourth century that first decreed the celibacy of the Catholic priesthood. The Reconquest, that protracted struggle of Christian against Muslim, represented for all Europe a struggle between good and evil, and knights from many countries came to fight in it: Sir James Douglas was killed in one of its campaigns, shouting 'A Douglas! A Douglas!' as he charged the Moors, and wearing the heart of The Bruce in a small casket around his neck. The Inquisition, as it developed in Spain under Isabel and Ferdinand, set a pattern of intolerance for the world, and is still remembered today, we may fancy, wherever there is a dank cell or a torture chamber. The War of the Spanish Succession changed the face of Europe. The Peninsular War took Wellington to Waterloo. The Spanish Civil War, when the Nazis obliterated Guernica and the Russians set up their secret police headquarters in Alcalá de Henares, not half a mile from Cervantes' birthplace – that nightmare was a pre-view or rehearsal of the world war that was to follow, and so bemused the impotent Powers of the West that Anthony Eden nicknamed it the War of the Spanish Obsession.

Spain does have a microcosmic quality, and this sometimes makes her people feel a kind of chosen race. Many Spaniards have Jewish blood in them, and Spain possesses some of the doomed, self-centred, inspirational quality of Jewry – a feeling not merely of isolation, but of vocation. It is not, however, anything divine. It is only the land, the wind, the sun, and the history. The master illusion of Spain is the conviction that the Spaniards are a people different, when they are only a people separate – that *alma* has made them so, when it is only geopolitics. Spanishness is as much a response as an impulse, and Spain is so Spanish because until now she has known little

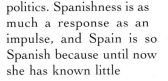

Café scene

else: because long ago she turned her back upon the rest of us, and thus prolonged not only many archaic miseries, but also many grandeurs and beauties of the human spirit. She made her own bed, in the brief years of her Golden Age, and she still tosses and turns in it.

Sancho thought it was an island because his master had always promised him one, and Spain too has long been an Isle Barataria: an island that is not an island, an island across the railway line, that thinks itself alone among the waters because Don Quixote says so.

2
PLURAL
SPAIN

East from Saragossa, near the road to Barcelona, stands the strange mountain of Montserrat, a pile of queerly serrated jags, bumps, and crevices which was hacked into shape by the golden axes of angels. It is one of the oddest of Spain's celebrated sights, so bizarre but refulgent in its outline in the sunlight, and it naturally possesses all kinds of meanings. For some it is the jolliest of afternoon outings, with its high mountain meadows to scatter wastepaper on, its several funiculars and its fragrance of pines. For many more it is the shrine of the Black Virgin of Montserrat, found miraculously in a cave up there, and now the centre of one of Spain's best-loved and liveliest cults.

But for others it represents chiefly the diversity of Spain, the centrifugal nature of this State: for Montserrat is the focus or emblem of Catalonia, one of several nations long since embedded in the side of Spain, but still recognizably masters of their own character. Montserrat could only be in Catalonia, the most endlessly energetic and ingenious of these old entities. It could exist nowhere else in Spain. It is a very holy place, but if you spend a night in its monastery hotel you will find that it is far from the sepulchral otherworldliness of the Escorial. On the contrary, it proliferates with earthy life. The pilgrims process energetically around the courtyard with their candles, singing the sweet hymn of Montserrat and led by jolly bearded friars. The eighty-four Benedictine monks of the establishment cross themselves in vigorous unison in the Basilica. The funiculars burst with

Montserrat

46

trippers. The young people up from Barcelona dance the *sardana*, a faunlike capering of Catalonia, in prancing circles outside the post office. Tourists happily meander through the souvenir shops, priests stroll in smiling pairs along the mountain paths, and often through the doors of the shrine comes the sickly music of the Montserrat choirboys, who have been singing in this particular way, in this particular place, for at least seven centuries. Montserrat has a bounce and a gusto that is all Catalan. It is unmistakably Spain, but Spain, the Catalans would say, plus. If you look at the table of pamphlets in the porch of the Basilica, you will find that one pile is in Castilian Spanish, but the other in the Catalan tongue.

Seven arrows in a yoke formed the crest of Isabel and Ferdinand, representing not only their own union in marriage, but also the union of Spain. Unity is an obsession in this country, if only because it is so precarious, and centralism *versus* federation is one of the perennial Spanish issues. To the Romans Spain was always plural, and even when the separate Spanish principalities were united, the Castilian monarchs still carefully called themselves *Los Reyes de las Españas* – Kings of the Spains. The old entities – León or Navarre, Asturias, Galicia, Aragón, or Catalonia – maintained their autonomy for centuries. They had their own parliaments, armies, civil services, and exchequers, and their legal systems were so trenchantly independent that to this day the *fueros* or public privileges of Aragón form an appendix to the Spanish civil code.

Inevitably the dangers of separatism have preoccupied the rulers of Spain. King Ramiro II of Aragón, faced with a rebellion among his subject lords, invited them all to Huesca to show them, he said, a wonderful new bell whose sound would be heard all over the country: when they got there, he decapitated them all and, placing fifteen heads in a circle to represent the bell rim, hung the sixteenth from a string to be the clapper. Isabel and Ferdinand, after the fall of Granada, firmly suppressed the power of the great nobles; and just to make sure that Aragón and Catalonia did not become economic masters of the kingdom, a codicil to Isabel's will decreed that no citizen of those two regions was to conduct any commerce in the New World. Since then successive rulers have tried to concentrate all power in Castile, the

A landscape
in Aragón

heartland of Spain – from Philip II, who made
Madrid the capital, to General Franco, a Galician
himself but a stern proponent of central government.

They never quite succeeded. The old kingdoms are still remembered
in the modern regional groupings of Spain – Galicia, León, Asturias,
Old and New Castile, Navarre, Aragón, Catalonia, Estremadura,
Murcia, and Andalusia; and in the provinces of the north, in particular, the yoke that binds the arrows always chafed. Guernica, that
symbolically tragic little town in Vizcaya, demonstrates how mystically
potent these old prides can be. It is a very small place, encouched in a
green valley among the hills, but for at least a thousand years it has
been the holy city of the Spanish Basques. The bomb-aimers of the
German Condor Legion did their best to destroy it for Franco in the
Civil War, but even now it still feels like the capital of some separate,
secret State. The Basques are the queerest and staunchest of the
Spanish minorities, a people that seem to have no relatives, and may be
the last remnant of the original Iberians. Their language is so complex
that a verb, for example, incorporates in its one word not only the pronoun but also the complement, so that each transitive has twenty-four
variations – 'he gives to you' is one word, and 'she gave to us' is

another. Their Catholicism is so dour and stolid as to be almost Calvinist in flavour. Their architecture is all blacks and whites and patterned walls. Their churches look like airship hangars, they invented the art of whaling, and their national game, *pelota*, is the fastest of all ball games.

The racial pride of this mysterious people has always revolved around the sacred oak of Guernica, beneath whose branches the laws of the Basques were promulgated and the Kings of Spain swore to respect their privileges. You may see it there still, and marvellously suggestive it remains of ancient right and loyalties. The bombing miraculously spared this part of the town, and the oak still stands in the shadow of the old Assembly House. You will find it beneath a little cupola in the garden, a stunted, shrivelled old thing, less like a tree than a kind of totem: and as you peer at it through the iron railings, with a stocky Basque gardener, perhaps, keeping an eye on you from inside, or a pair of housewives gossiping in incomprehensible polysyllables behind your back – as you look at this rather uncanny old relic you may feel how forceful are the emotions that it inspired in the past, emotions that lie beneath the tragedy of Picasso's famous picture, and are still a thread in the texture of Spain.

These northern peoples have always felt themselves stifled or exploited by the Castilian centre of Spain. They feel that they provide an unfair proportion of the State's brawn and brainpower – that they are more advanced than Castile, more enlightened, more European. Most of the nation's industry is in Catalonia, Asturias, and the Basque country, and much of Spain's contemporary intellectual ferment is occurring among the Catalans. The only properly modern big cities in Spain – cities, that is to say, comparable to the metropoles of the industrial West – are Barcelona and Bilbao: the one a rip-roaring,

Guernica

furious, and sometimes dangerous Mediterranean seaport, the other an exceedingly well-ordered sort of Hamburg. Driving into Barcelona from Valencia or Saragossa is like passing into a different civilization: the road sweeps into town through smoky plants and resplendent glasshouses, there are great buildings all about you, and pompous Parisian boulevards, a port full of foreign ships, an overhead railway lurching across the harbour, noise indescribable, pressure intense, a passionate, avaricious, tireless feeling in the air – and all the way along the approach road, like the frenzied motels that guide you into an American city, straggles a parade of garish camping-sites, evidence of the truth that Barcelona is always looking outwards, northwards, over the frontier, to where the new things come from.

No wonder the centrifugal instincts of the Basques and Catalans have proved irrepressible. Before the Civil War both provinces had their own autonomous governments, Catalonia actually constituting a separate republic within the Spanish State. Franco suppressed them, but failed to destroy the old patriotisms that lay behind. Throughout his rule the Basques maintained their own Government in exile in France, and the moment he died both they and the Catalans demanded the restoration of their old rights, sometimes constitutionally, sometimes in violence.

The other regions, too, began to chafe at the centralism of Spain, and demanded some degree of independence – even the Canary Islands had their nationalists – and the new Spanish democracy pledged itself almost from the start to devolution of one sort or another. For the Basque and the Catalan extremists, of course, nothing but absolute separatism will suffice. More probably Spain, so long obsessed with the unity of authority, will loosen itself one day into a federal State, recognizing rather than repressing the separate styles of its several ancient entities; and perhaps in the end this redistribution of power will prove to be the most distinctively Spanish contribution to the progress of the nation-states.

Spanish loyalties are subdivided, too, for Spain is not merely a regional country, but a passionately local one as well. To many Spaniards, patriotism goes no farther than the village, and Spain in the abstract is only a tax-collector or a sergeant-major. The Spanish language varies not only from province to province, but actually from village to village, and so self-contained is the village entity that in the Napoleonic Wars the Mayor of Móstoles, a hamlet near Madrid, personally declared war on France. The strength of the dominant Castilian culture clothes this country in a common patina, but beneath the yoke and the arrows it is a place of astonishing diversity.

Spain, the microcosm, is always evoking somewhere else, partly because Spain has set her seal upon so much of the world, partly because of her own immense variety. She is the kingdom of exceptions, where every generalization must be qualified, and every judgement half reserved. What is true of part of her is seldom true of another. What seems to be a national characteristic turns out to be only a village custom. When the fruit is falling in the south, the blossom is budding in the north. There are hardly any mules in the Basque country, but hundreds of thousands in Andalusia. There are hardly any bull-rings in the north-west, but every southern village has one. In Andalusia the houses are blazing white and red-tiled, in Aragón they are mud-brown and flecked with bits of straw. In Asturias they build their grain stores with tiled eaves and stilts, to keep the rain and the rats out. The Basque policemen wear red berets, the men of La Mancha wear headscarves and ride about in covered wagons like Western pioneers. The churches of Valencia have blue tiled domes, the fences of Galicia are made of upright stone blocks, every part of Spain has its own traditional costume, pictured in flurries of ruffles and pleated petticoats in all the best tourist brochures.

In the Levante live the people of the lagoons, rice growers and eel fishers; in Asturias the miners look like Glamorgan men in clogs; in Andalusia rich gypsies inhabit caves with two storeys and refrigerators. In Catalonia you are almost a Provençal, honouring the familiar values of southern Europe; in Andalusia you are a

La Alberca

52

Garrovillas,
Estramadura

kind of African, smouldering with gypsy blood and freely relieving yourself, if twelve years old or under, on the front door step of your own house. The people of La Alberca, a famous tourist village near Cuidad Rodrigo, are said to be Swabians, and sit in their narrow cobbled lanes looking pinched and secretive, as though they are expecting dark news from Bavaria. The people of the moorlands near Astorga are Maragatos, a stocky race of muleteers, whose origins are unknown and whose thirty-six hamlets, strung out drearily across the flatlands, look like railway villages along some abandoned English branch line.

This is still a country of local specialities: wines vary widely from town to town, and so do foods. In San Sebastián they make small pastries designed to look like ham and eggs. In Toledo they make marzipan. Oviedo is famous for its stews, richly compounded of vegetable broth and black pudding, and Vigo for its eel-pies. Segovia is the place for suckling pigs, their forlorn little carcases spread-eagled pink and spongy in the restaurant windows. Seville is the home of *gazpacho*, a delicious cold soup of cucumber, tomato, and miscellaneous garnishings. In Estremadura they feed their pigs on snake-flesh to improve the quality of the ham. In Aranjuez, near Madrid, they will offer you the best strawberries in Europe, served with a little orange juice and ripe in early March. Only in Catalonia can you eat a proper *zarzuela*, a gargantuan fish soup; in only one Spanish town – Soria – have I ever been given fresh-water crayfish. Uniformity has not yet fallen upon Spain, and towns often retain a sense of guild: this one makes paper, this one lace, this one swords, this one cars, this one wooden figures of Don Quixote, and the little town of Jijona, near Alicante, makes nothing else but nougat. 'Local in everything' is how Richard Ford described the Spaniard a century ago; and though his horizons have clearly widened since then, parochial loyalties can still be so fierce that more than once the pious devotees of one village Virgin have crept out at night and destroyed the sacred image of the Virgin down the road.

Even Spanishness itself, *casticismo*, the quality that binds the nation and makes its flavour instantly recognizable – even this is tempered by the provinces, and has its lights, shades and distortions. The archetypal Castilian has to him something of the gaunt meditative quality that El Greco gave to his saints, or Velázquez to his Hapsburgs: his eyes are deep-set, his expression is concentrated, and whether he is jogging to a shack on a big mule, or stepping into a night club out of an Alfa-Romeo, he looks as though he is pursued by some mighty preoccupation. This grave model is coarsened by the Catalans, dullened by the Galicians, solidified by the Basques, and parodied by the flamboyant Andalusians. To the haughty Castilian, the people of the provinces spring from lesser breeds – 'south of the Ebro Africa begins'; and if you watch some jaunty Sevillian walking along a street, and compare him with the image of this noble norm – if you superimpose the Andalusian upon the Castilian style, you will begin to see why. Into the sad eyes

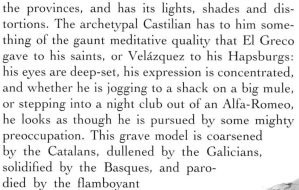

A landscape between Almería and Vera

A view of
Montserrat

there steals a hint of hilarity. Into the stately step there intrudes a flamenco beat. That air of tremendous meditation is replaced by an exhalation of ceaseless charm. The impeccable Castilian intonation is slithered and slurred, the solemn courtesy is laced with bonhomie, and in the very harmony of the Andalusian presence the Dorian seems to be replaced by a syncopated Phrygian mode. The Andalusian is a Spaniard still, a Spaniard unmistakable; but in the context of *casticismo*, some Spaniards are distinctly more Spanish than others.

For when we think of Spain, we think of Castile, with its peers of the high *meseta*. For some the other provinces may be Spain plus; for me they are always Spain minus. It is in Castile that the proper magic of Spain resides, casting its spell from Finisterre to Almería, and projecting its familiar image to the four corners of the world. It is not, I think, either a tolerant or a talented country. Its manner is autocratic, often domineering. Its landscapes are cruel and its climate is terrible – nine months of winter, says the proverb, three of hell. But as we wander through the narrative of this book, around the wide perimeters of Spain, so we shall feel ourselves looking always over our shoulder to the stern splendours of the interior: just as sometimes up at Montserrat, when the echoes of the *sardana* are wheezing reedily beneath your window, or the gay little waitresses are giggling at the kitchen door – sometimes in the Catalan fizz of it all you may pine for that other country to the west, so aquiline and lofty, and wish you were there in some grand old city of the tableland, musty among its steppes, with a cadaverous grave waiter to bring you your garlic soup, and Philip II, with Torquemada and El Greco, dining silently at the next table.

3
LADY
OF ELCHE

South of the Ebro', the traditionalists sneer: but it was not so far south of the Ebro that the most splendid ancestor of *casticismo* was interred and resurrected. Near Valencia there stands a town called Elche. It is indeed half African in temper. Around it there straggles the biggest palm grove in Europe, a phenomenon whose dates are not of the best quality, but whose palm fronds, weirdly tied together in bunches on the tree, and thus whitened through lack of sap, are in demand all over Spain because of their well-known powers of protection against lightning. Elche is a low, square-built, flat-roofed, whitewashed, unprepossessing place; but in the shade of its palm forest in 1897, they dug up one of the most celebrated busts in the world, *La Dama de Elche* – the Lady of Elche, carved by an unknown artist at least twenty-five centuries ago, and now, on her plinth in the Prado Museum in Madrid, looking more *castiza* than ever.

She is a formidable dame: a broad-shouldered, rosy, heavily built woman, slung about with amulets, with an elaborate cartwheel head-dress and a general air of no-nonsense, as though she is about to tell a recalcitrant nephew to pull himself together, or ask some wilting cousin where on earth she bought that frightful dress. She looks as though, if there were more to her than head and shoulders, her arms might well be akimbo. In her steady and accusatory gaze, however, I

The palm grove, Elche

58

El Pilar, Saragossa

like to fancy you can see
the beginnings of the
Spanish artistic taste, as
it has been immortalized
in the pictures, the
buildings and the litera-
ture of this fitfully fertile
country. The Lady of Elche, who is plainly Iberian with strong Greek blood, is representational,
to be sure – vividly, rather alarmingly so. But she is truth slightly
heightened, clarity with a shot of mescalin: and much of the art that
has succeeded her down the centuries, like the society itself that gave
birth to it all, has this quality of being lifelike, but more so – intenser,
taller, more vertical, perhaps more real than reality.

Its basis is clarity, for this is the first characteristic of Spain. Here all
is *sol* or *sombra* – sun or shade, as they call the two halves of the bull-
ring. You are seldom halfway in Spain. It is either fearfully hot or
frightfully cold. You are either a good man or a bad one, either very
rich or very poor, either a faithful church-goer or an out-and-out dis-
believer. The light is brilliant, the atmosphere is preservative, the
colours are vivid – so vivid, for all the vast monotony of the *meseta*, that
sometimes this seems like a painted country, as the mauve and purple
shadows shift across the hills, as the sun picks out a village here, a crag
there, as the clouds idly scud across the candlewick landscape of olives

or cork oaks, and the red soil at your feet seems to smoulder in the heat. It is no accident that the Spaniards are masters of the art of flood-lighting. They learnt the skill from nature, and it is a splendid thing to see one of the great buildings of Spain illuminated suddenly by sun or lightning against this background of fugitive colour – the grand tower of Segovia, say, standing suddenly among the cornfields, or the exotic domes and towers of Saragossa, resplendently alone beside the Ebro.

Intellectually Spain is similarly unequivocal, and expresses herself well in the long analytical stare that often greets the stranger in Castile. The shape of Spain is symmetrical, and the Spaniard likes everything else to conform. He distrusts loose ends and anomalies. *Limpieza*, purity, is one of the great Spanish abstractions. Spain does not, like the oyster, turn her grit to pearls: she merely spews it out. Jews, Moors and gypsies have all been expelled from this kingdom in the cause of purity, and the world is generally full of Spanish exiles. Some three hundred thousand people left Spain because of the Spanish Civil War: Picasso, Balenciaga, Casals, Salvador de Madariaga were all exiled pieces of Spanish grit. The Spaniard likes things to be final, and emphatic. Even the Spanish exclamation mark exclaims twice, thus: *!Caramba!* – which is to say, in our milder vernacular, Goodness me! (though as a matter of fact this legendary Spanish expletive is rarely heard nowadays, and has perhaps reverted to its other dictionary definition, 'an ancient headgear for women'). No wonder absolutism has been the *leit-motif* of Spanish politics. 'Do you forgive your enemies?' a nineteenth-century Duke of Valencia is asked on his deathbed in a famous Spanish anecdote. 'I have no enemies,' he retorts, 'I've had them all shot.'

Everything must be definite, positive, cut-and-dried. Castilian itself, besides being one of the most phonetic of all languages, is one of the most subtly precise, and the sages of the Spanish Academy are constantly polishing its idioms. Spain is a country of polarities – it used to be maintained among the Spanish Jesuits, indeed, that the human body being magnetic, if you placed a corpse in a big enough bath its head would swing around to north. The endless proverbs of Spain, so dear to Sancho Panza, are nearly always of a dry, succinct kind, revolving to very obvious conclusions: and *Don Quixote* itself is so graphic in its symbolisms that without much simplification it can be retold as one of the best of all children's stories. The mystics of Spain have often had a universal appeal: St. John of the Cross, that whole-hog little ascetic, whose poems can still move the most truculent agnostic, or St. Theresa, such a saint as every small girl, during her religious phase, would give her favourite pony to emulate; or even St. Ignatius, the Basque soldier, who once tested God's will by allowing his mule to decide whether or not a disputatious Moor should be killed – 'if the beast goes right, I spare him, if it goes left, he dies'. The intellectuals known as the 'generation of ninety-eight' (Cuba fell in 1898, and with it the last pretensions of Spanish imperialism) couched their ideas in language as catchy and easy to understand as advertising copy – 'I feel a mediaeval man in me', 'Spain hurts me', 'Nothing if not a man', 'We love Spain because we do not like her'. Federico García Lorca, who was murdered in 1936 and buried in an unknown grave, foretold his own fate in a remarkable instance of this exact and explicit kind of mysticism:

> *Then I realized I had been murdered.*
> *They looked for me in cafés, cemeteries and churches . . .*
> *but they did not find me*
> *They never found me?*
> *No. They never found me.*

The Spaniard likes to be sure. The monotony of the *corrida* lies in the fact that the bull always loses, but to Spanish minds this is essential to the drama, just as death is essential to life. Philip II, wishing to be absolutely certain, lived surrounded by dossiers, and you have only to visit a Spanish Government

Lorca

department today, stagger past its endless bureaux and be guided through its networks of dockets, cross-references, lines of authority or channels of responsibility, to know that the Spaniard still revels in the minutiae of bureaucracy. He loves to have everything tabulated: when the Bishop of Ciudad Rodrigo was murdered at his desk during the Civil War, his assassins looked at his papers to see what he had been doing, and found that he had been sorting out his 13,400 card references to the History of Toledo. Castles, caves, and churches all have street numbers in Spain, and every Spanish cathedral has upon its façade a mark showing its altitude. Upon one of the gates of Burgos there is a dim scratch, in the shadow of the arch, which romantics variously interpret as indicating the length of the Cid's sword or the arm-span of that hero as a monstrous babe-in-arms, but which certainly is, whatever its original purpose, a sign of the Spaniard's immemorial passion for measuring things. Spanish roads are among the most carefully and intelligently signed in Europe. Spanish traffic policemen, though their style greatly varies from town to town, or perhaps from mood to temperament, are nothing if not lucid: with a snap or a click of muscles they halt you, white gloves beneath white sun-helmet, or with a Wagnerian sweep they wave you on, and sometimes they ornament their gestures with little grace-notes of traffic control – like the man to whom Mr. H. V. Morton once gratefully tipped his hat, and who responded by removing his helmet and bowing.

Spanish bookshops are full of multi-volumed, heavily indexed, neatly tabulated tomes about the structure, organization, flora, literature, geology, economy, communications or Women of Spain, and the Spaniard has actually managed to whittle away at geography with his enthusiasm for neat ends – the colonies on the other shore of the Mediterranean, Ceuta and Melilla, have long been metamorphosed in the Spanish official mind into integral parts of the peninsula. Often the papers will tell you that the hottest place in Spain yesterday was Tenerife, in the Canary Islands, seven hundred miles out in the Atlantic. The cities of Spain are often wonderfully tidy and close-knit, and the ports of Spain often look like model harbours in a museum. A quaint example of this toy-like exactitude of Spain is the royal palace at Santander on the northern coast, built for Alfonso XIII by public-

subscription: it stands upon a little spit, halfway between the port and the bathing beaches, and looks like a child's idea of a palace, its castellated mansion nicely on the summit of the peninsula, its stables and servants' quarters properly disposed about its flanks, surrounded on three sides by the sea and on the fourth by loyal subjects. There is nothing cloudy or crooked to Spanish arrangements. The structure of syndicates, or official trade unions, established by Franco's Government was actually called a vertical system: the pillar of consultation began with the worker, rose neatly through management and ownership, and ended at the top, oddly enough, with General Franco.

I once asked a lighthouse-keeper at Algeciras how he liked his job, and he replied unexpectedly that it was *muy romántico* – very romantic. If logic can be touched with rhapsody in Spain, so much the better – the official name for the old part of Madrid is the Romantic Quarter – and if the dramatic solution can be reached with a proper formality, it is always worth seeking. I once reported a theft to the criminal investigation department of Barcelona, a resolutely smoky, shabby, Maigret-like place, with a pair of detectives playing chess to an attentive audience of colleagues, and a smell of ink, tobacco, typewriters, and old clothes. They listened to me carefully, took down my deposition in triplicate, and threw open a door into an inner room in which, they fondly supposed, my stolen goods were displayed upon a table. A dejected young villain was already snuffling in a corner, awaiting my arrival; the policemen led me to the table with proud struts of achievement; but alas, the goods were

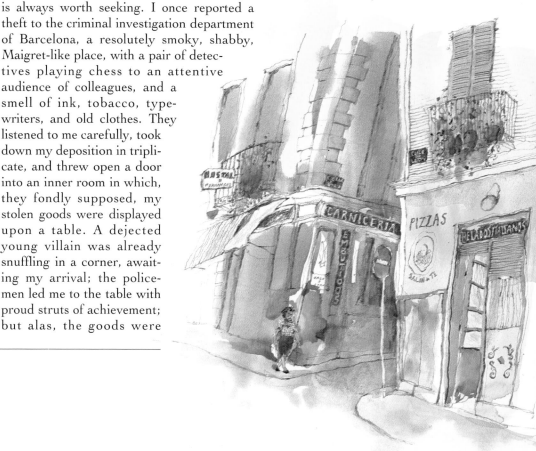

The Romantic Quarter, Madrid

somebody else's, victim could not be confronted with culprit, and the detectives seemed so disappointed at the failure of the *coup de théâtre* that even the chess game flopped, and I left them morosely putting the pawns away in a cardboard box.

Spain prefers the all-or-nothing. She is an *etched* country. The acid in her life makes the picture dignified but preternaturally distinct, and she is torn always, as her own writers have a tendency to tell us, between two tremendous poles – Man and Universe.

So it is a kind of towering realism, spiced with the caustic, that characterizes the most typically Spanish art – that partnership of Quixote and Sancho, or St. Theresa's 'God among the saucepans'. Even before that Lady of Elche, the cave artists of Altamira were painting deer that looked like deer – but a little lither and lovelier than they would be on the hoof. The great Spanish painters usually talk in a language that we all understand; and even when they are immigrants to Spain, nevertheless that language is generally the pure and stately vernacular of Castile.

If it is El Greco the Cretan who is painting, the idiom is tinged with something mystical and searching, expressed in a lengthening of feature and a sad uniformity of expression: all El Greco's men have virtually the same face, and it is a face so absolutely and unmistakably Spanish that you may see it still today wherever the Castilians have left their mark. If it is Velázquez at work, then the extra dimension is at once more human and more pathetic: the officers of *The Lances*, some watching the formalities of surrender, some glancing at the painter, with looks of proud melancholy detachment; or Prince Baltazar Carlos on his plump pony, who ought to be having a splendid time, but somehow, at seven years old, already looks weighed down by the burdens of princeship; or the little Infanta of *Las Meniñas*, never alone, always watched – by her proud parents, by her doting ladies, by the court chamberlain at the door, by the jester and the female dwarf and the grave kind artist himself, the eye of the world.

If it is Goya who is painting, then the foreshortening goes another way, and mankind is made stumpier and coarser than life: the figure of

The church of San Antonio de la Florida, Madrid

St. Anthony, in the Church of San Antonio de la Florida in Madrid, is so prosaic that although he is in the act of raising a man from the dead, at first you do not notice him at all among the gay figures of the frieze. The family of Charles IV, in the most famous and enigmatical of all royal portrait groups, looks as though its members have been squashed in some kind of satirical press. The tragic figures of 1808 rising against the French look less like patriotic heroes than aborigines, all mop-hair and thick limbs. The ghastly figures of Goya's 'black paintings', the cannibalistic Saturns, flying witches, and monsters, look to my eye all too down-to-earth, as though they are unfortunate entries in a fancy dress competition.

Even the great modern Spaniards – Picasso, Dali, Miró – sometimes express a similar swollen realism. No picture ever had a more instant and universal impact than Picasso's *Guernica*, in all its tangled horror, and when we look along one of Dali's silent Catalan beaches it is as though we are seeing our own favourite holiday cove infinitely extended, infinitely hushed and littered with things like giraffes and trombones that we might well have seen for ourselves, if we had been luckier with the weather.

No less in sculpture does the Spanish artist make you feel that the thing is familiar, but divinely ennobled. Spain is endlessly rich in suggestive statues, from the gently smiling figures of the Virgin to be found in every other cathedral – a little wry, a little self-deprecatory – to the celebrated figures of Quixote and Sancho in the Plaza de España in Madrid, the old knight riding his Rosinante with such an air of command that the Communists used to say his outstretched hand was directing them to storm the prison, while the Nationalists claimed it was giving the Fascist salute. Up the road, near the Royal Palace, the equestrian figure of Philip IV, the best horseman in Spain, is a stirring example of the *genre*: Velázquez designed it, it was cast in Florence, the mathematics of its construction are said to have been worked out by Galileo, and it stands there so gloriously lifelike that even now you almost expect it to wheel around with a whinny and a toss of its mane, and make for the next jump.

There is a seventeenth-century figure of St. Bruno, in the monastery of Miraflores at Burgos, so disconcertingly realistic that somebody once said of it that 'if he weren't a Carthusian he would certainly speak'. There is a figure of Goya in the cathedral plaza at Saragossa, which is attended by four stone admirers, giving it an extraordinary feeling of immediacy: they are a charming, summery group of young people, in cravat and crinoline, disposed at a respectful garden-party distance on the lawn. There is a figure of the Cid, beside the River Burgos, whose tremendous romantic gusto almost halts the passing traffic: a giant of a man, on a great bronze brute of a horse, with his cape flying like wings in the wind behind him, and his eyes beneath the iron helmet trained ferociously upon an unseen army across the bridge. And best of all are the royal monuments of Spain: the cold grand effigies of the Catholic Monarchs in Granada Cathedral, guarded by the most sumptuous of screens and surveyed by birds with gilded beaks; or the superb alabaster figures of Juan II and Isabel of Castile, in the Miraflores at Burgos, carved with exquisite grace and humour by the great Gil de Siloé; or Philip II, breathtakingly lifelike, kneeling erect with his family in the chapel of his own Escorial: memorials, all of them, that marvellously reflect the mystic nature of kingship, its claim to be something grander and more privileged than nature.

The Spaniard has been, in some periods of his history, a master of the ornate styles, which he has often made his own – in particular, the wilder extravagances of Baroque (a mode which the anarchists of the Civil War were particularly fond of, because it burnt so well). The style called plateresque, in which stone was worked like folderols of

The gallery of the College of St Gregorio, Valladolid

silverware, or the later aberration called Churrigueresque, after a family of craftsmen whose numbers are not known, but who seem by the profusion of their work to have been beyond the reach of any census – these expressions of exuberance, one reflecting the sudden richness of the Renaissance, the other the aspirations of the Counter-Reformation, are a speciality of Spain. Sometimes they are undeniably invigorating. There is a small town called Priego de Córdoba, in the northern part of Andalusia, which contains some very prodigies of Spanish Rococo, and enchanting they are to find, tucked away in a fold of that lofty landscape – a municipal fountain spurting merrily through a hundred jets, churches encrusted everywhere with tumbling cherubs, whirligigs, gilded leaves, comical manipulations of sunshine and perspective, gigantic plaster set pieces, alcoves, scalloped niches and naves of such cosmetic elaboration that they look less like ancient shrines than stations on the Moscow underground. The Sacristy of the Carthusian monastery in Granada, a marvel of Churrigueresque, looks as though its decoration has been not carved, nor even daubed, but rather squeezed out of a tube. The celebrated plateresque façades of Valladolid strike me as being, when one has recovered from the riotous shock of them, actually edible.

They are Spanish indeed, and for some they may represent Spain best of all; but for my tastes they are too flippant, too frothy, and their practitioners stand in relation to the masters of Spanish austerity as a gifted interior decorator might stand to the engineer of a pyramid.

For the Spanish art *par excellence* is building – not architecture simply, but the art of designing a structure, relating it to its surroundings, and erecting it so that the very act of its construction, the very way it sits on the ground or holds up its buttresses, is an excitement and an inspiration. This is the vertical art, the right-angled aesthetic, and thus it best suits the Spanish genius. The Spaniards, helped and taught by numberless Frenchmen, Germans, Flemings, Italians and Englishmen, were the greatest builders between the Romans and the Americans, and wherever they ruled they left noble works of masonry behind them.

Most of their best buildings smack of engineering, from the rough cyclopean walls of Tarragona, one vast boulder laboriously heaved upon another, to Antonio Gaudi's astonishing Church of the Sagrada Familia in Barcelona, which was unfinished when he died in 1926, and stands there now like a vast spare part for some gargantuan machine. The Spaniards are good at the big, strong things: dams, ships, heavy trucks, canals, roads. The Romans left some hefty items in Spain – the fine old lighthouse at Corunna, for instance, which is still shining, or the mighty aqueduct at Segovia, which still conveys the city's drinking

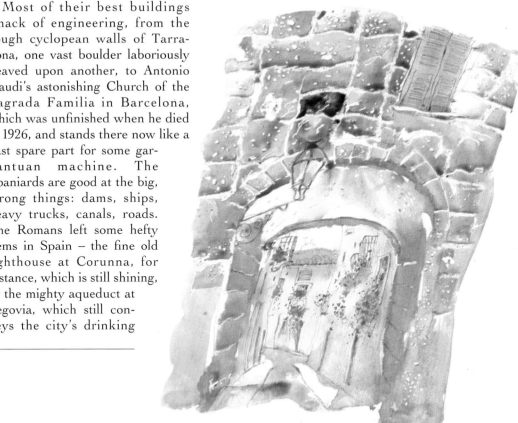

The walls of Tarragona

water. The Spaniards followed their example, and their country is full of virtuoso engineering. The one-aisled Catalan cathedrals, Palma or Gerona, are staggering in their vast vaulted spaces – forerunners of the immense railway stations of the Victorian age, just as the glass-fronted buildings of Corunna foreshadowed the airy skyscrapers of Manhattan. There is a twelfth-century church at Santiago de Compostela which, unless it has been twisted into its present form by subsidence or earthquake, is an extraordinary structural *tour de force*: all its pillars lean outwards at a dizzy angle, giving the impression that the whole building is about to bust apart at the roof, or that you are seeing it in a distorting mirror. And if you have any doubts about the strength of Spanish construction, take a close look at the cathedral of Ciudad Rodrigo, which was in fact knocked sideways by an earthquake in the last century, but still stands there solidly enough, skew-whiff but intact.

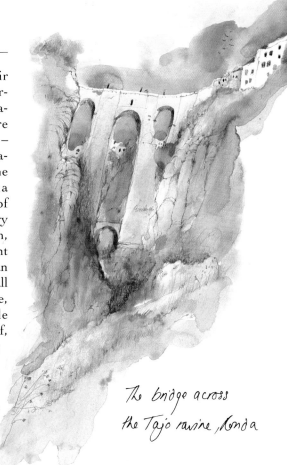

The bridge across the Tajo ravine, Ronda

Nothing expresses the sober strength of Spain better than bridges – more numerous than you might suppose, in a country with so few rivers, because of her corrugated terrain. Scarcely a Spanish town cannot boast a fine bridge. Sometimes it is a discreet little gem of a thing, no more than a few paces long, neatly embellished with statuary above a non-existent stream. Sometimes it is an object of imperial stature – the sixty grave arches of the Roman bridge at Mérida, which King Erwig the Visigoth repaired, or the two fine structures, one new, one old, that carry the traveller from Portugal across the Guadiana into Badajoz. The small humped bridges of Spain, Roman or mediaeval, across which the sheep-flocks are so often to be seen shoving each other in a tumult of heaving white wool, pursued by the shrill cries of the shepherd boy behind – those ubiquitous little works are often of a splendid strong simplicity, springing from rock to rock with an almost organic ease. The ornamental bridges that cross the moat-like River Turia at Valencia form a delectably graceful corona for that rather lumpish city. The celebrated bridge across the Tajo ravine at Ronda, which has a restaurant in the former prison cell above its central arch, is one of the most spectacular sights in all Spain: below it the gorge plunges a sheer five hundred feet, and deep down there in the shadows, as you sip your coffee high above, the river bubbles most disturbingly.

The bridges of Spain play a significant part in the history and folklore of the country. It was upon the slightly wiggly old bridge over the Orbigo at Veguellina, in León, that a famous tournament was held in 1434 – precisely the kind of event that Cervantes was mocking in *Don Quixote*. A preposterous knight-errant, wearing an iron chain around his neck as token of his love-enslavement, stood upon the bridge with nine colleagues and challenged every passing unfortunate to deny that his lady was the most beautiful on earth. Seven hundred and twenty-seven passers-by were silly enough to contest this proposition, all of them were instantly engaged in combat, several were badly hurt, and one actually died. The castellated bridge of San Martín at Toledo is the subject of

The bridge of San Martín, Toledo

71

another famous story. Almost at the moment of its completion, we are told, its designer confided to his wife the awful truth that he had made some errors in his calculations, and that as soon as the scaffolding was taken away it would almost certainly collapse. The resourceful lady saved her husband's reputation by stealing out that very night and setting fire to the thing, thus enabling the engineer to start all over again from scratch, and build his span so stoutly that it is still as good as new. Spain is a paradise for the lover of bridges: even now they are building them all over the place, and one of the more tantalizing things in the peninsula is the presence near Zamora of the Cabriles railway viaduct, for many years the largest concrete span on earth, but so inaccessible that to have a good look at it you must either row for several miles across a reservoir, or pull the communication cord of your passing express.

As with bridges so with churches – the same pleasures of strength and purpose, whether they are gracing a corner of some great city or dominating the whole being of a tumbled hamlet of the steppe. In their combination of form and faith they really do express, more than most churches, the conception of God as the master-scaffolder. The Spanish church-builders never much liked airiness or fuss, except in decoration: the quality that most of their best works share is one of devout muscularity.

For many people the most satisfying of them all are the ancient churches of the north, some the unique products of the Visigothic kingdoms, some Romanesque – the latter reflecting in their severe and sinewy simplicity the spirit of Romanesque that ran clean across southern Europe, and the influence of the Cluny Benedictines who brought to Spain their own brand of ordered and efficient Christianity. There are several famous pre-Romanesque buildings – notably the two robust little churches, all on their own on a hillside, which stand so silent and deserted on the road above Oviedo, looking down like cowled monks themselves upon the industrial tumult of the city below. And there is nothing more powerful than Spanish Romanesque, when you encounter it not in the shape of a great cathedral, Zamora, Santiago, or Lugo, but in some damp green-enfolded hamlet of Cantabria – all flowers and freshness in the spring, all gentle drizzle in the winter. You bounce up a bumpy lane to get there, perhaps, with high banks to obscure your vision, and when at last you reach the village, so bold upon the signpost at the road junction, it turns out to be only a cluster of two or three small houses, deep in the fields. Proudly on the hill above it, hardly bigger than a house itself but formidable beyond its scale, there stands the church: its arcade like a little market place, where you expect to see the merchants lounging, its apse like the rounded poop of an old ship, where the captain might be looking through his telescope, its reddish bulk squat and compact, its interior formal, cool, and massive. Finding this sophisticated structure there among its meadows (wistaria creeping up the priest's house outside, flocks and pansies in the churchyard) is like knocking at the door of some sweet spinster's cottage and finding it occupied by a mathematician of international authority – such is the force of the style, and such its quiet distinction.

Lugo Cathedral

The Moors, too, were engineers of great skill, and there is nothing wishy-washy to the sacred buildings they erected in Spain: some in a pure Islamic kind; some in the style called Mozarabic, which was developed by Christians under Muslim rule; some in its reverse, Mudejar – Muslim and Christian Gothic mingling after the Reconquest. The interior of the Alhambra, that delicate symbol of Muslim decadence, looks more like a boudoir than a king's headquarters, and a voluptuous excess seems to have characterized the vanished palace of Es-Zahrâ, outside Córdoba, which the Caliph Abder-Rahman III built for one of his favourites, and fitted out with several zoos and a bedroom pool of quicksilver. The mosques of Spain, however, were generally more

The Giralda Tower,
Seville

virile memorials. We can still see, through a Christian overlay, the warlike simplicity of the great mosque at Córdoba, so near the desert in its tent-like forest of supporting pillars, so faithful to Mahomet's tenets of cleanliness, abstinence, and regularity in its marching symmetry, its squareness, the fountains playing among the orange trees in its courtyard and the tall minaret that stands like a prod to the conscience above its gate.

The massive pink tower of the Giralda above Seville Cathedral is one of the supreme monuments of Muslim engineering, comparable only to the minarets of Rabat and Marrakesh in Morocco (it used to be said that all three were built by the same architect, the brilliant Jebir; but unfortunately it has lately been demonstrated that there never was such a person). It is absolutely square, a gentle ramp takes you to the top of it, it is faced with glazed tiles, and at night-time, when the floodlights pick it out, big eagle-like birds, bleached by the light, sail and waver eerily around the angel on its summit.

Such towers – some built as mosques, some as churches after the Reconquest – are to be found all over Spain, and many of the most haunting of them are in the north-east, where the hold of the Moors was relatively brief. This is because, during periods of intolerance in Muslim Spain, many Christian refugees fled northwards, taking with them the skill and tastes they had learnt from Islam. Thus one of the great surprises of Spain is the octagonal tower of San Pablo in Saragossa, obvious godson to a minaret, which is suddenly revealed in its slender brick splendour in one of the narrowest, scruffiest, and noisiest squares of the city. And of all the half-Moorish towns of Spain, perhaps the most evocative of Africa and Arabia is Calatayud, a day's drive from France, in the heart of Aragón. It is partly the summer heat that makes it so, and the dust, and the emptiness of landscape; and partly the dun crumbled mountain that rises behind the town riddled with the burrows of troglodytes, crowned with the wreck of a fort, and looking as African as any Atlas or Mokattam; but it is chiefly the minarets that stand above the rooftops of the place, lording it over its cramped streets – spiky, slim, rather arrogant, and looking so bravely Muslim still that you can almost hear the click of the muezzin's loudspeakers in the dawn, and see the white-robed figures hastening to their ablutions. Such buildings of infidel inspiration, left behind like a sediment, powerfully contribute to the flavour of Spain, and remind us always of her collateral desert origins.

And so to the great cathedrals, Romanesque, Transitional, Gothic, or Renaissance, which are the flower of the Spanish constructions, and which for the world outside generally epitomize the Spanish presence. As the skyscrapers are to New York so are the cathedrals to Spain: Avila, Barcelona, Burgos, Granada, Jaén, León, Málaga, Murcia, Palma, Salamanca, Santiago, Saragossa, Segovia, Seville, Toledo –

Murcia Cathedral

masterpieces every one, and supplemented in every region of Spain by lesser structures that would be, in any other country, national brags themselves. They are museums too – the first of the public collections – and treasure houses, and repositories of Spanish history, and lively agencies of the tourist industry, and places of ancient pilgrimage, like Santiago de Compostela, or of public assembly, like the cloisters of Barcelona (where the civic tittle-tattle is exchanged on Sunday mornings, and the sacred geese waddle about their pond with a fearfully knowing air). In the porch of Valencia Cathedral the farmers' representatives meet each Thursday morning to approve, in formal caucus, the current distribution of irrigation water. In the cloisters of Zamora Cathedral there is kept, in a shimmer of rich colour and mediaevalism, one of the most dazzling collections of tapestries in Europe.

Every fair-sized Spanish town has a cathedral. Saragossa and Salamanca have two each. Madrid has been building one on and off since 1623, and has got as far as the crypt. Some are essentially genial – Murcia, for instance, whose tower was compared by Richard Ford to a drawn-out telescope, and which is pre-eminently a jolly, sailor-like, benevolent old structure. Some are more like fortresses than holy places, especially the military cathedrals of Catalonia – and above all Palma, the most magnificent expression of the Catalan spirit, which stands foursquare on its ramparts above the harbour, the very champion of Majorca, the first thing to challenge you when you reach the island by sea, and the last you can see over your shoulder when you drive away into the mountainous interior.

Málaga Cathedral

76

Some are, more than anything else, *big*: the Renaissance cathedral of Jaén looks preposterously out of scale in that middling category of city, and the Gothic cathedral of Seville is defeated, in the grandeur stakes, only by St.Peter's in Rome – 'Let us erect such a grand temple,' said the canons of the chapter when they decided upon its construction, 'that we shall go down to posterity, if only as madmen.' Some are just plain self-satisfied: Málaga, which has only one completed tower, and stands there like a much-decorated one-armed general, or Segovia, which has to compete for attention with a white fairy castle along the ridge, and is all too aware that it wins.

Let me pluck two buildings from these stupendous ranks, as colour-sergeants to represent them all. Let us first follow the pilgrim route to Santiago de Compostela, the Galician city immortalized by its legendary association with St. James – Santiago means St. James. In mediaeval times this city was outclassed only by Jerusalem and Rome as an object of Christian pilgrimage, and no palmer's collection of trophies was complete without the scallop shell of Santiago (worn on the hat, in those days, rather as today's pilgrims stick a picture of the Grand Canyon on their rear window, or flutter all over with souvenir pennants as they hitch their hikes to Oberammergau). It is a small city, neatly bunched in the Virgilian countryside of Galicia, all cows, straw hats, and haywains; and you are scarcely within its perimeters, have scarcely sniffed the civic odour of sanctity and tourism, before you have emerged from Calle Franco – Franco Lane – and are in the cathedral square.

It is still, as it was for those ancient pilgrims, one of the great moments of travel. The square is immensely wide, and seems to be made of golden granite. In front of you there stands, euphonious of name and princely of posture, the Hostal de Los Reyes Católicos, founded by Isabel and Ferdinand as a hostel for pilgrims, and now perhaps the most beautiful hotel in Europe. To the left is the Renaissance pile of the Prefecture in whose basement cells there are probably languishing a few not very desperate prisoners. Cars seldom cross this celestial plaza, but pedestrians are always about – tourists, hotel pages, policemen, priests; and surveying the calm but never torpid scene, which has a Venetian quality of depth and movement, stands the tall façade of the cathedral, unquestionably one of the great buildings of the world. It is like nowhere else. At one end of its enormous block there rises a pyramidical tower of apparently Hindu genesis. In front of its great door two staircases rise so jauntily from the level of the square that they seem to be leading you to some blithe belvedere. And in the centre of the composition the twin west towers of the cathedral soar into the blue in a sensational flourish of Baroque, covered everywhere with figures of St. James in pilgrim guise, crowned with balls, bells, stars, crosses, and weathercocks, speckled with green lichens and snapdragons in the crevices, and exuding a delightful air of cheerful satisfaction.

The interior of this happy building is basically Romanesque. A glorious carved portico is its western entrance, telling the story of the Last Judgement in meticulous stonework, supervised by Our Lord and his Evangelists, attended by angels, patriarchs, and abashed monsters, and having at its base a kneeling figure of the cathedral's mastermason, Maestro Mateo. A glittering statue of St. James, all gems and silver, stands above the high altar, and all day long a stream of pilgrims climb a little staircase to kiss its mantle. The aisles are lined with confessionals, each for pilgrims from a different country – in the heyday of this shrine an average of five thousand pilgrims came to Santiago every day between Easter and Michaelmas. On feast days there swings from the roof a gigantic censer so heavy that it takes six men to set it in motion, and when it once got out of control it hurled itself clean out of the door. I know of no building with more fizz than this long-beloved cathedral, and I wholeheartedly sympathize with the old superstition which still, to this hard-boiled day, makes educated men touch foreheads with that figure of old Mateo, to gain from the bump some small portion of his talent.

Very different is our second great fane, the Gothic cathedral of Burgos. Burgos is a political city – the home of the Cid, the ancient capital of Castile, General Franco's capital during the Civil War – and its cathedral too has to it a feeling of profound temporal consequence. There is no fun or flare to Burgos Cathedral. Its exterior is all grey solemnity. Its two grilled towers, gun-metal colour, look like the lattice-work masts of old American battleships. Its north door is always locked – to prevent the citizens of Burgos, so the guidebooks say severely, using the cathedral as a public throughfare. Grim grey steps lead you to the main doors; forbidding vergers jangle their keys inside; all through the cathedral darkness lies, like smoke or night-time. Burgos Cathedral is French in architectural origin, but nothing in Spain feels more Spanish. There looms the great *coro*, black and square, and through the twilight there coruscate, wherever you look, wonderful shining or fretted things – huge golden grilles, gilded staircases, figures of saints, kings, or heroes, reliquaries in silver frames, vast and glorious reredoses, canopies, cupolas, the mitres of dead bishops and the banners of victorious kings.

In the Condestable chapel, beyond the high altar, there lies upon his splendid tomb Don Pedro Hernandez de Velasco, Hereditary Constable of Castile, who died in the fifteenth century, but whose marble thick-veined hands still warily grasp his sword-hilt. In the chapel of Santísimo Cristo hangs the miraculous Christ of Burgos, supposed to have been fashioned by Nicodemus, made of soft buffalo-hide and real hair, emaciated, tragic and so lifelike that in the old days it used to be thought its fingernails had to be manicured. High on the wall of the sacristy stands the rusty old iron-bound chest called the Coffer of the Cid, which that resourceful warrior once filled with sand and pledged to some gullible Jews as a chest of gold. Burgos is a gnarled, dour, idiosyncratic

Burgos Cathedral

79

building; and when you leave its gloomy old purlieus, wander down to the pleasant riverside gardens of the city, or drive away up the hill into the bare countryside all about, it remains in your memory not as a joy, nor even an inspiration, but as an iron glower in the mind.

Sometimes the sharpness of the Spanish style goes sour or muzzy – just as the clarifying drugs, if taken to excess, end by making you either muddled or megalomaniac. There is much that is ugly in Spain, and there is a good deal that has taken a step over the frontier of reality, and feels half crazy.

For all its beauties it is a Philistine country. Switch on your radio, as you drive away from Burgos, and you will find its programmes drowned in raucous commercialism. Stroll down to the fine old theatre, when you stop for the night, and you will almost certainly find it closed for lack of support: virtually the only theatres left in the Spanish provinces are the ramshackle plaster-and-canvas stages of the travelling players – a company of whom once told me, at their muddy stand outside Vich, that their two most popular productions were *Peter Pan* and *La Dame aux Camélias*. Turn off your light when you go to bed, and you will find the night hideous with the hootings, exhaust roars and loud voices of a society that has not yet adapted itself to the machine age, and actually prefers noise. Cast around for a bookshop in the morning, and if you find one at all it will probably be the sort that hides its limited literature behind a selection of sunglasses, china matadors, and postcards of Andalusian beauties with revolving plastic eyes. The church music of Spain is usually screeching, saccharine, or *fortissimo*. The universities are only now recovering from the impositions of a repressive Catholicism and an intolerant neo-Fascism. The Inquisition's narrowing of judgement or intellectual initiative is still apparent in Spain, and there is a depressing shortage of properly educated, generally cultivated men and women – what in other countries of the West constitutes 'the reading public'. The educationalist Francisco Giner tried to create such a class in the nineteenth century, and the generation of 1898 was the brilliant nucleus of one, but the Civil War put the Philistines in command, and the artists, writers, architects and

The palace of Charles V
in the Alhambra, Granada

publishers of Spain are only now recovering their verve.

This is nothing new. Spanish architecture, in particular, has often been impelled by vulgar motives – the desire to go one better or, more pertinently, one bigger. It was Charles V who, in 1526, deposited in the middle of the Alhambra the gigantic circular palace now named after him, crudely disrupting the precious frivolity of the place. It was the same king's royal council that sanctioned the building of a cathedral in the centre of the great mosque at Córdoba – against the fervent wishes of the local municipality, which bravely declared that the work destroyed in the operation 'could never be replaced by anything of such perfection'. The fantastic Churrigueresque sacristy of the Carthusian monastery at Granada, and the vast cathedral humped up against the Giralda at Seville, were patently demonstrations of the Christian ability to build bigger and more elaborate buildings than any old infidel. The exquisite Transitional cathedral of Salamanca was dwarfed in the sixteenth century by the enormous mass of the new cathedral that was built beside it – intended to proclaim not so much the glory of God as the fame of Salamanca University. The Spaniards are perpetually erecting huge and awful figures of Christ, to dominate the sweet hermitages and shrines of earlier generations, and though their best restorers are among the most skilful in Europe, their lesser practitioners seem constitutionally incapable of leaving well alone.

The Spanish taste for strong leadership has done much to vulgarize the scene. The Escorial rises far above rhetoric, if only because of its fanatic dedication, but Franco's Air Ministry building down the road in Madrid, so lumpish, so grandiloquent – such a building is a very proclamation of autocracy's habitual mediocrity. Spain is littered with such tasteless monuments – the writhing symbolisms of innumerable war memorials, vast and sanctimonious seminaries, the indescribably dreadful Labour University at Gijón, the barrack-like hostels erected by the syndicates on the ski slopes above Madrid. The exquisite balance of Toledo has been upset by a huge military college on the other side of the river. The evocative little cave of Covadonga, where Pelayo the Visigoth, we are told, fought the battle that began the Reconquest – that haunting shrine in the heart of the Asturian mountains has been overwhelmed by a grandiose Basilica built across the valley. A massive convent has tarnished the best view of Avila; a bishop's palace built by Gaudi, like a cardboard ogre castle, stands grossly

The Archbishop's palace, Astorga, built by Gaudi

beside the pleasant cathedral of Astorga. It is almost as though the Spaniards deliberately try to disturb the equilibrium of the scene, to seize your attention by shocking your sensibilities, and make your hackles rise.

This is a disagreeable aberration from the Spanish norm – so decorous, so discreet, so sober. Much more attractive is the turn the genius takes when, sated at last with so much logic, it takes off into fallacy, and presently confuses the fanciful with the true. 'Absurdity,' the historian Angel Ganivet once wrote, 'is the nerve and mainstay of Spain.' This is the country of picaresque, whose eccentrics are usually likable and whose gamblers are always optimistic – 'Patience and reshuffle', says the Spanish proverb gaily, calling for a new pack. Legends, myths, and fairy tales line the chronicles of Spain, and Spaniards cherish a strong taste for a dream-like kind of make-believe – most creepily embodied, perhaps, in the gait of the Bigheads, those swollen puppet-heads which Spaniards put on at fiestas, so upsetting the normal balance of their locomotion that they have to walk around the town in a peculiar rolling, strutting movement, like figures in a nightmare – this one a witch, this one a policeman, this one a painted old harridan with a fly as big as a mouse upon her nose.

You would expect to find such oddities and hallucinations in Galicia, where the Celtic strain is strong, and where wee folk, poltergeists, and the smell of brimstone are all familiar; and indeed one of my favourite examples of Spanish second sight concerns the shrine of St. James at Santiago. The Galicians will readily tell you why the shrine is there. St. James the Greater, they say, preached the Gospel in Spain soon after the Crucifixion, and after his martyrdom in

The shrine of St James, Santiago de Compostela

Jerusalem his body was smuggled back to Galicia by a party of Spanish disciples. During the sea voyage its miraculous presence saved the life of a man who had been carried out to sea by a frightened horse, and since both man and beast were found covered with scallop shells, the scallop became the badge of St. James and of the Galician pilgrimage. All this, the Galicians say, is well known. The sarcophagus was lost for several centuries, but a star revealed its whereabouts – Compostela means 'field of a star' – and there the city of Santiago was built. St. James was a great traveller, they will tell you, which is why he is often portrayed as a pilgrim, and a great warrior, which is why he is often portrayed on horseback, smiting black infidels with a sword.

But in all this, alas, they are deceiving themselves, and for the stranger it has become exceedingly difficult to sort out fact from Santiago fancy. St. James, so all the best scholars seem to agree, never came to Spain at all. He was never a soldier. There is no earthly reason why his body should be brought to Galicia, and nothing of the sort is suggested in the Acts of the Apostles, where his death is recorded. He died several centuries before Islam was conceived, probably never mounted a horse in his life, and certainly never slew an infidel. If his emblem is a shell, it is probably because he was a fisherman by trade. If he is pictured with a pilgrim's staff, it is because the sculptors, years ago, mixed up the cause with the effect, and confused the saint with his supplicants. There is no historical reason why Santiago should be a place of pilgrimage, why the cunning monks of Cluny should have fostered its international reputation, or why that joyful shrine should exist at all. It is only an illusion; but so long has it been in the Spanish mind, so attractive is it in itself, that long ago, in the way of all the best hallucinations, it achieved a kind of truth.

This is, of course, the essence of Quixotry. 'The Character', as they call him in Spain, was crazy – but in his craziness he expressed great truths. To this day an aura of hazed reality surrounds the name of Don Quixote in Spain, for just as the Galicians have convinced themselves that St. James fought the Muslims at Santiago, and Londoners look in all seriousness for 221B Baker Street, so many Spaniards take it for granted that Don Quixote actually existed. I once stopped my car in the colourless expanses of La Mancha, the knight's homeland, and asked a couple of ploughmen which of the villages I could see around me was in fact Don Quixote's birthplace. 'Don Quixote de la Mancha?' said they, for they always give him his full title, out of respect. 'Why, he was born just outside Argamasilla de Alba. They've pulled the house down, but you can still see the place – over there, señor, beyond the church tower, that's where Don Quixote de la Mancha was born!'

They had no doubt about it: for just as the Character himself had no doubt about the windmills, so Spain sometimes likes to rise above the brilliant sunlit clarity of her landscapes, and peer into the mists above. Down here it is stately dames with arms akimbo. Up there the knights and saints ride by.

4
SOL
Y SOMBRA

We are in the Spanish South. The castanets click from coast to coast, the cicadas hum through the night, the air is heavy with jasmine and orange blossom, the soil is rich red or raw desert, there are prickly pears at the roadside, the girls have black eyes and undulating carriages, and often there hangs upon the evening the sad but florid strain of *cante jondo* – the 'deep song', part Oriental, part Gregorian, part Moorish, part Jewish, that the gypsies have made the theme music of the south.

For half the world the image of Spain is the image of Andalusia – the huge slab of country, mostly mountainous, that begins where the table-land is bounded by the southern sierras. Eight Spanish provinces make up Andalusia. Almería, in the extreme south-east, is an Andalusian city, and so is Cádiz, in the far west. Andalusia contains the highest mountain in Spain, the hottest shoreline, the teaming tourist resorts of the Costa del Sol, the fine old cities of Seville, Granada, and Córdoba, the ports of Málaga and Cádiz, the handsome mountain town of Ronda, Jerez de la Frontera, where the sherry comes from, and Vejer de la Frontera, perhaps the most spectacular of all Spanish villages.

Andalusia is romantic Spain, popularized by Gautier, Mérimée, Bizet, and Washington Irving, and still dangerously bewitching. The very name of the Alhambra stands for courtesans and silver slippers. The very sight of the Seville tobacco factory sends one off humming the Toreador Song. The very glimpse of a bull-fight poster from Torre-molinos, taken home by some eager tourist and stuck upon a living-room wall – the mere glimpse of those gaudy

The Tower of Gold, Seville

colours, with their memories of *pasodobles* and seafood in the evening, sums up the romantic allure of Spain, and makes the citizen of the dank north fret for his summer holidays. To the Moors, Andalusia was an earthly paradise. To the travel agents it still is. To the rest of Spain it stands in rather the relationship of some flibbertigibbet but undeniably charming cousin – of whom indulgent elders say you really needn't worry, John's the kind that always falls on his feet.

But to all too many of the Andalusians themselves, this is a homeland less than Arcadian. Andalusia is *sol y sombra* both – sun on one side of the street, shadow on the other: a mirror both of Spain's delight, and of her lingering poverty.

It is only fair to look first at this profligate in a winning streak, for the overwhelming characteristic of Andalusia is charm, and the glummest of sociological analysts could scarely drive through its countryside without enjoying himself. As you descend to this lotus-land down some winding highway through the Sierra Morena, Andalusia lulls you at once into susceptibility. There lies the first of her villages, down in the river hollow, with a fine old bridge to take you there, and a lofty old church awaiting your arrival. There is a thread of smoke on the air, and a smell of fat from the breakfast batter they are cooking in the streets, and on the river bank a few early risers are already scrubbing their sheets beside the water. In you go, down the whitewashed cobbled streets, and all around you there seem to be flowers – in pots affixed to outside walls, in neat little gardens, in patios glimpsed through the grilled doors of houses.

Such a place often looks like a set in some old-school Ruritanian musical, and its inhabitants, too, move against these delightful backdrops with a stagy air. Here are all the stock characters of the Spanish legend: the leathery muleteer, his string of animals heavy with sacks, panniers, or baskets of vegetables; the Murillo boy trotting by on his donkey, all tousled mischief; the swanky landlord's agent in his flat Córdoba hat, one hand elegantly at his hip, on a grey mare with a fancy saddle; the women chattering perpetually around the fountain, their big water-pots propped upon its parapet; the village grocer, glimpsed dimly through a curtain of hanging hams, garlics, and sausages; the staunch old beldame, all in black, whitewashing her house with a bundle of sticks for a brush; the silent shepherd with his goats and sheep, jostling each other down the street; the miller in his windmill on the ridge, with a smell of flour, a creaking of old wooden mechanisms, and two caged partridges on a wall; the gamblers playing dominoes and inexplicable card games in the café; the priest, and the pair of Civil Guardsmen in their grey capes and patent-leather hats, and the busybody official watching your arrival from a municipal window, and the comical village policeman in his white helmet, his face a very picture of bucolic bonhomie.

Of course there are motor-bikes too, and cars, and television aerials, but still the old image is true. Andalusia gloriously lives up to its reputation, and is as full of colourful vitality as any opera stage; full of hard work, as the labourers pursue their archaic skills in the fields; full of gossip and curiosity and the music of unseen radios, as the cheerful children swarm about your car, and the old ladies in shawls gaze at you unwinking from the doors of their houses. There are no half-measures in such a place, so close to the earth, so perilously near the frontiers of caricature. You feel that its people have already made up their minds, after some deliberation: having decided not to cut your throat, for the dramatic effect, they are, with a policeman's salute and a wave from the shrouded grocer, altogether at your service.

Such is romantic Spain at its roots. To see it at its flowering climax, you should go to the famous Feria of Seville, which takes place in April, and is at once so unusual, so entertaining, and so beautiful that few other fairs in the world can match it. The old city warms up to the event for some weeks in advance. The great fairground, down by Carmen's tobacco factory, is prettied up with flowers and fairy lamps. The proud families of Andalusia, the clubs, the syndicates, and the livelier commercial firms, erect their tented pavilions along the boulevards. The hotels, cautiously doubling their prices for the occasion, rent out their last upstairs back rooms. The whole rhythm of the city is accelerated, the pressure is intensified, the streets are crowded, the cafés hilarious, magnificent horsemen clatter through the city centre, the stranger feels that some civic blood-vessel is surely about to burst —

The Feria, Seville

       and finally, early in April,
all this happy fever detonates the
annual explosion of the Feria.

It is part a parade, of horses, fashions, and handsome citizens. It is part a binge, where people eat and drink all night, and dance into the morning. It is part an entertainment, where the best dancers and musicians of Andalusia come to display their talents. It is part a mating session, where the best families gather to share reminiscences, swop prejudices, and introduce eligible nephews to likely nieces. In the morning there takes place the most brilliant of all Spain's *paseos* – a *paseo* with horses. Hour after hour, in the warm spring sunshine, the Andalusians ride up and down that fairground – to see and be seen, look each other's dressage up and down, and inquire after the dear Marquis. The married and the very young ride by in lovely polished carriages, drawn sometimes by the proudest of mules, sometimes by pairs of elegant Arabs, and just occasionally by that prodigy of the carriage trade, a five-in-hand. Their coachmen are sometimes decked up in gorgeous liveries, turbans, toppers, Druse costume or tam-o'-shanters, and often some winsome grand-daughter perches herself upon the open hood of the barouche, her frilled white skirt drooping over the back.

As for those of marriageable age, they trot up and down those boulevards like figures of Welsh mythology: two to a horse, the young man proud as a peacock in front, the girl seductively side-saddle behind. He is dressed in all the splendour of the Andalusian dandy, the tightest of jackets and the most rakish of hats, looking lithe, lean, and possibly corseted; she wears a rose in her hair and a long, full, flowering, flounced polka-dot dress – blue, pink, mauve, bright yellow or flaming red. Never was there such a morning spectacle. The old people look marvellously well fed and valeted; the coachmen are superbly cocksure; and sometimes one of those courting couples will wheel around with a spark of hoofs, the beau reining sharply in like a cowboy at the brink of a canyon, the belle clutching his shapely waist or holding the flower in her hair, to mount the pavement to some gay pavilion, the horse snorting and the lovers laughing, and accept a stirrup cup from a smiling friend.

In the evening the binge begins, and the fairground, blazing with flags and lights, becomes a stupendous kind of night club. The air is loud with handclaps and the clicking of castanets, and all among the huge ornamental buildings that flank the fairground, with their ponds, parapets, and courtyards, groups of young people are dancing in the shadows – sometimes suddenly swooping, like so many flocks of chirping birds, from one corner to another, from one alcove to the next, or helter-skelter over a hump-back bridge to the other side of the water. The bright pavilions of the fairground streets now sizzle with celebration – bands thumping, dishes clashing, families deep in gossip over their drinks, gypsies cooking ghastly greasy stews outside tents of sybaritic silkiness, stolid railwaymen listening to the music, or groups of children, resplendent in their southern fineries, dancing stately measures on a stage. Sometimes you hear a hoarse flourish of *cante jondo*, from some gypsy virtuoso hired for the evening. Sometimes the young bloods come dancing by, arm in arm across the pavement, with a transistor to give them rhythm, and feathers in their hats. Everywhere there is the beat of the flamenco, the clatter of heels and castanets, the creak of carriage wheels, the smell of horses, the swish of romantic skirts, and the noise, like the shuttle of distant looms, of twenty thousand clapping hands.

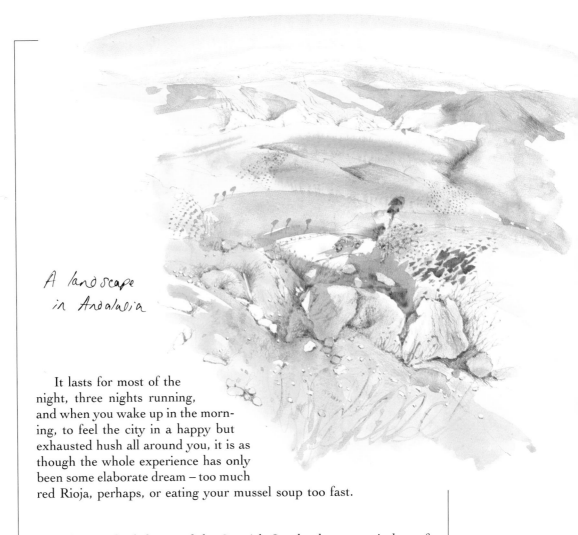

A landscape
in Andalusia

It lasts for most of the
night, three nights running,
and when you wake up in the morning, to feel the city in a happy but
exhausted hush all around you, it is as
though the whole experience has only
been some elaborate dream – too much
red Rioja, perhaps, or eating your mussel soup too fast.

It is the standard dream of the Spanish South, the romantic bag of
tricks. If you are only on holiday, it is enough – few regions on earth
today can offer you so much fun, so much excitement, so much sponta-
neous beauty. But to see the other face of the Andalusian mirror, you
must turn away from the dazzle of Seville, and look for a moment at
a statistical map. Of the ten poorest provinces in Spain, five are in

SOL Y SOMBRA

Andalusia: there are only two Andalusian provinces that reach the mean level of Spanish prosperity. This is the country of the great estates and the landless peasantry, and it is here, all among the orange blossom, that we can best remind ourselves of the poorness of Spain.

For despite her air of grandeur, she is not a rich country. Her moments of prosperity have been transient. The Romans and the Moors both brought her some prosperity, in the days when her land was less eroded. The Incas and the Aztecs willy-nilly enriched her, in the days when the gold of the Americas poured convoy by convoy into her coffers. Before the Spanish Civil War she still possessed the sixth largest gold reserve on earth – mostly frittered away during the conflict in buying arms from the Russians. She is, though, one of the generically poor countries. It used to be thought that her unexploited reserves of minerals – iron, copper, bauxite, manganese – were virtually limitless, and had only to be released from their seams to make her rich again. Now the experts are more cautious. There is plenty of hydro-electric power in Spain, and plenty of low-quality coal, but there is no oil at all, and most of the other deposits are apparently too skimpy to allow much industrial expansion. The first Spanish industrial revolution, bravely launched by the Basques and Catalans in the early nineteenth century, never quite sparked: to this day the industries of Spain are largely confined to three small areas – Madrid, Catalonia, and the Cantabrian coast, where the Basques and Asturians live. Spain has never properly adjusted to the technical era. She does not have the carburettor touch, and the only Spaniards who treat a car with any finesse are the meticulous street thieves of Barcelona.

Spanish agriculture, for all the space of its landscapes and diligence of its peasants, can only just produce enough food to feed the population. Spain is self-supporting in that mystic trio of foodstuffs, wine, wheat, and olives, which is the traditional staple of a Mediterranean diet; in a bad year, however, she already has to import other foods, and her population is increasing faster than her agricultural production. Sixty per cent of Spain has never been cultivated, and never will be – half the soil of Andalusia, the geographers say, has been blown into the sea. Of the rest, much is cultivated with archaic inefficiency. Many farms have been split so many times, in the course of family inheri-

95

tance, that they are now almost farcically fragmented. Sometimes a hundred acres is divided into a couple of thousand plots and distributed among two or three hundred owners, and there are olive trees in Spain that have been distributed branch by branch among brothers. The one-cow farm is a commonplace in Galicia, where the farmer's wife may often be seen leading her entire livestock on a string. On the other hand the vast *latifundios* of the south, estates on a South American scale, are too immense and unwieldy to be efficient: the landlord usually lives far away, in some comfortable apartment of Madrid or Seville; the agent is often corrupt, usually ignorant, and seldom enlightened; the landless peasants labour on, generation after generation, with no incentive but the stark need to survive. Hundreds of thousands are obliged to go abroad to get work at all, and there is a ceaseless migration out of the countryside into the towns. The markets of Spain are often such miracles of lush fecundity, so cherry-red and corn-rich, that it is difficult to realize how harsh a life Spain offers all too many of her countrymen, how constantly they must struggle against climate, social structure, and terrain, and how enormous is the gulf that divides visitor from villager.

For Spain is full of hardship – do not be deceived by the smiles, the elegant clothes, the ubiquitous aerials and the slum clearance. Men of the Spanish bourgeoisie, teachers, bureaucrats, or army officers, often have two separate jobs to make ends meet, and even the overwhelming love of children that is so characteristic of Spanish life stems partly from the fear of poverty, for one day those boys and girls, so prettily indulged today, will have to support their aged parents. There is no more heart-rending experience than to spend a morning with a team of Spanish sardine fishermen on a bad day; they work like slaves, wading into the sea with their huge net, laboriously hauling it, inch by inch, hour by hour, up the sands: so much depends upon that catch, so much labour and good humour has been expended, so courteous are those men to one another, so many hungry children are waiting to be fed at home – and when at last the catch appears, a dozen small fish in the mesh of the net, a sensation of hopeless resignation seems to fall upon the beach, and the fishermen, carefully clearing up their tackle, separate to their homes in weary silence.

All this you may sense most pungently in Andalusia, if you get off the main roads and keep your reactions sharpened. The worst is over now, as modernity creeps into the south; down on the coast the glittering blocks of the tourist towns are very symbols of change and chance; but this is a country only just escaping from indigence, and there are abject corners still. Only within the last couple of decades have Andalusian country people been introduced to running water, lavatories, domestic electricity, tractors. Many village streets are still made of earth – cloudy dust in the summer, impassable when the rains fall. In thousands of village houses cocks, goats and even pigs share living quarters with the owners. The children look much healthier nowadays, but the last generation's poverty is everywhere to be seen – women aged beyond their years, men mis-shapen, blind or mindless.

Sometimes even now this poverty is so primitive that you have to rub your eyes or blink to make sure that you are in Europe at all. The cave-dwellings of Andalusia, for instance, though generally comfortable enough, are sometimes little more than burrows: if you wander

Torremolinos

through the great cave-city of Guadix, east of Granada, which rises like a huge warren among the hills above the town, you will find that the lower caves are nicely whitewashed and pleasantly furnished, lit by electric light, with bright curtains at their entrances, flowers on their trellises, and demure women sewing at the tables of their little patios. Go further up the hill, though, through the maze of lanes and cave-terraces, and presently you will find those tunnels getting dirtier, and darker, and crumblier, and more lair-like, until at last, in the ashen slopes high above the town, some wild covey of slum children will come swooping out of a crack in the ground, so wolfish, swift and swart that you will turn on your heels instinctively, and fall headlong down the hill again.

And most elemental of all are the strange thatched huts, more hay-stacks than houses, that you still see here and there in Andalusia, like kraals in the African veldt. I was once most kindly entertained in one of these homesteads – a pair of huts, side by side, with living quarters in one and sleeping quarters in the other. Nothing could be simpler, or much nearer the lives of our neolithic forebears. An open fire burnt in the centre of the living hut, and everything inside seemed charred or blackened with smoke. The hut-people had no beds to sleep on, only a pile of blankets; they had no schools to go to; they lived, so far as I could make out, on soup and bread; and when I stumbled over a sack upon the ground, I heard a faint but testy squeak beneath my feet, and discovered that it contained a small black pig. Those Spaniards possessed, I think, not one single inessential – not a picture, not an ornament, not even a ribbon for the hair. They could not read, they had no wireless, and they had never seen a city. They were, as nearly as a European human can be in the twentieth century, animals.

But animals of dignity. I asked the father of the family if he liked his way of life, and his only complaint was

Guadix

Near Tordesillas, on the road to Santiago

the inflammability of the huts — they were *always* burning down, he said. The Spaniard bears his poverty without much grievance, so that the visitor, overwhelmed by the flourish of it all, scarcely notices how poor the people are. Indeed, life is undeniably improving, as modernity creeps in: most villages have electric street lighting nowadays, and there can hardly be a row of houses in Spain that does not possess a television. Your conscience will not always niggle you, as you wander through Andalusia. It is a tactful kind of Paradise. You will be able to convince yourself, easily enough, that half the poor prefer to be poor, and the other half won't be poor much longer.

For one must admit that the earthiness of Spain, which is the cousin of backwardness, is often very beautiful to experience. One of the glories of Spain is her bread, which the Romans remarked upon a thousand years ago, and which is said to be so good because the corn is left to the last possible moment to ripen upon the stalk. It is the best bread I know, and its coarse, strong, springy substance epitomizes all that is admirable about Spanish simplicity. It is rough indeed, and unrefined, but feels full of life; and poor Spain too, as you may see her in Andalusia, seems crude but richly organic. Some of her vast landscapes have still never felt the tread of a tractor. All has been tilled by hand, and all still feels ordered and graceful, the energies of the earth rising in logical gradation through ear of corn or trunk of olive into the walls and crowning towers of the villages, sprouting themselves like out-crops of rock from the soil. Spain is a hierarchal country: on the farm, from the grave old paterfamilias at one end to the turnips in the field at the other; in the nation, from the grandees of Church and State, the brilliant young men at the Feria, or the debutantes showing their knees in the noisy sports cars of Madrid, to those simple people of the thatched huts, with their huddle of blankets on the earth floor, and their piglets in sacks beside the fire. It may not be just, the *sol y sombra*, it is inevitably changing, but it feels all too natural: just as the bread, though it may lack finesse, certainly fills you up.

5
ALIENS

Cante jondo, I observed a few pages back, is part Oriental, part Gregorian, part Moorish, part Jewish, and is best sung by gypsies. I was, however, oversimplifying. Some authorities detect Phoenician origins in this archetypically Spanish music. Some fancy echoes of Byzantine liturgy. Some hear the rhythms of the African Negroes, and some castanets of Troy. There never was such a palimpsest as Spain, so layered with alien influences. From the tiers of the Roman amphitheatre at Sagunto, the *casus belli* of the Second Punic War, you may see the memorials of five different cultures: in the hillside above, the holes of the Iberian troglodytes; in the country around, the vines of the Greeks; beneath your feet, the Roman paving-stones; behind your back, a rambling Moorish castle; and away at the water's edge, the tall black chimneys of a blast furnace. Spain is the most militantly insular of States, but she is trodden all over with foreign footsteps.

The Great Mosque, Córdoba

How much is Moorish in the national temperament, and how much indigenous Iberian, the experts seem unable to decide; but there are moments, when the harshness of Spanish life feels particularly oppressive, when one is tempted to call everything abrasive Iberian, and everything lubricant Moorish. Certainly there are nagging undertones of regret to the greatest of the Islamic monuments of Spain, the Great

Mosque of Córdoba, for now that its mihrab has been demoted to be a mere curiosity, its courtyard taken in hand by the canons, its huge martial expanse blocked by the Christian altars in the middle, its old brotherly arcades walled in, its ablution fountains converted to ornamental pools, and its wandering sages banished for ever from the orange trees – now that it has been Christianized for seven hundred years, it feels a marvel *manqué*, a Dome of the Rock drained of its lofty magic, or a Kaaba removed from Mecca. It is only lately, under the example of foreigners, that the Spaniards have really recognized the Moorish genius – Unamuno, indeed, thought the Moorish conquest the supreme calamity of Spain. The Alhambra was used by the conquering Christians as a debtor's asylum, a hospital, a prison, and a munitions dump, and it is only in our own times that they have placed upon the ramparts of that golden fortress the haunting appeal of De Icaza's blind beggar:

> *Dale Limosna, Mujer,*
> *Que no hay en la vida nade*
> *Come la pena de ser*
> *Ciego en Granada.*

> *Alms, lady, alms! For there*
> *is nothing crueller in life*
> *than to be blind in Granada.*

The last Moriscos, or Christianized Moors, were expelled from Spain in 1609, but all over this country you will see people in whom the Moorish blood still runs – swarthy, skinny men built for the burnous, women whose eyes peer at you obliquely out of narrow windows, scampering small boys like Kasbah urchins, old men with

The Great Mosque, Córdoba

fringed beards like marabouts. There are no longer, as there were before the Civil War, women in the south who veil their faces like Muslims; but time and again, when some old village lady wanders into the grocery store and spots a stranger there, you will notice that she takes the corner of her black headscarf between her teeth, and holds it there defensively – precisely as the women of Egypt, midway between purdah and emancipation, half veil themselves in reflex. The Spaniards do not ride their donkeys in the rump-seated Arab manner (though the Spanish knights of the tourneys did adopt the short stirrup of the Moors); close your eyes one day, all the same, when some blithe donkey-man is passing your window, and as the neat little clip-clop of his hoofs echoes down the street, and as the man hums, half beneath his breath, some complex quarter-tone refrain, you may almost think yourself in Muscat or Aqaba, watching a portly merchant of the *suk* plodding through the palm groves.

The timeless quality of Spanish life still feels very Muslim: at the frontier with Andorra, any hot weekend, a Spanish frontier official sits on a kitchen chair in the sunshine to examine the passports, and looks so thoroughly pasha-like, with his papers and his paunch, that you actually notice the absence of his hubble-bubble. The Spanish talent for enjoyment sometimes reminds me of the Arab countries: like the Egyptians, the Spaniards love public holidays, public gardens, picnics, lookout towers, rowing incompetently about in boats or trailing in vast family groups through scenic wonders. The deadpan face of Spanish politics sometimes evokes visions of reticent sheikhs, and the Spanish passion for sweet sticky cakes has something to it of houris, harems, and jasmine tea. Now and then the guidebook will tantalizingly observe, of some small village in the Ebro delta, perhaps, or a remote high *pueblo* of Andalusia, that its people 'still preserve certain Moorish customs'; and though the book is never more explicit, and the village, when you reach it, usually seems all too ordinary, still the phrase may suggest to you, in a properly Oriental way, hidden legacies of magic, pederasty, or high living that make the East feel pleasantly at hand.

For the Moorish way of life was not confined to any conquering elite. The Moors impregnated the whole of society with their manners, so that even now it is easy to imagine the black tents of the Bedouin pitched, as once they were, around the walls of Toledo. During the centuries of the occupation, all Spain was bilingual – even the Christian princes of the north spoke Arabic to each other, and decked themselves in Moorish fineries. The Cid fought sometimes for a Christian faction, sometimes for a Muslim, and throughout the campaigns of the Reconquest there was constant intercourse, if only through the medium of refugees, between one side and the other. Many Christians were converted to Islam. Many more, though they kept their Christian faith under Moorish rule, looked, lived, and probably thought like Moors. The Muslims were rulers in Spain for more than seven centuries, and they dug their roots deep.

The gardens of the Portal in the Alhambra

There is a place in Granada that well demonstrates how deep. On the hill above the city there stands, of course, the Alhambra – foppish within, tremendous on the outside, especially if you pick out its red and golden walls through the lens of a distant telescope, and see it standing there beneath the Sierra Nevada like an illumination in a manuscript. The building I have in mind, though, is less grandiose. It stands in the heart of the town below, and to reach it you walk down a small alley beside a bar, and push open a great studded door on the right-hand side. There you will find, tucked away from the traffic, very quiet, very old, a Moorish caravanserai. It is a square arcaded structure, with a stone-flagged court, and its walls are so high that it is usually plunged in shadow. A caretaker family inhabits one corner, and the woman may look out at you from her kitchen window, pushing the hair back from her eyes; but the courtyard itself is nearly always deserted, and feels peopled only by ghosts. Nothing is easier than to see the merchants there, with their baggage-trains and their striped blankets, their hookahs and their towering turbans. Nothing is easier than to hear the racket of their bargaining, the shouts of the caravan-masters and the grunts of their animals, the liquid flow of Arabic among the elders squatting beneath the arcade, or the lovely intonation of the Koran from some blind beggar beside the gate.

And when you leave the place, to pop into the bar, perhaps, for a glass of wine and a plate of prawns, unexpectedly you will find that the ghosts have come with you, that the man behind the bar looks, now you think of it, remarkably like a Yemeni, and the hubbub of voices in the saloon behind your back is not at all unlike the haggle of a Syrian bazaar. It was not long ago. It is not far away. You can often see the houses of Morocco from the hills above Gibraltar, and Spain still possesses two enclaves, Ceuta and Melilla, over there on the Maghreb shore. In the Alpujarra mountains the godmother, returning the child to its parents after a christening, still says: 'Here is your child: you gave him to me a Moor, I hand him back a Christian.' When in 1936 the Nationalists besieged in the Toledo Alcazar were relieved at last by Franco's Army of Africa, they knew their ordeal was over because, listening through their battered walls to the noise of the streets outside, they heard the Moroccan infantry talking Arabic.

I was once loitering through Cádiz, that old white seaport on a spit, when I came across a boy and a girl playing soldiers. The girl was dressed as a knight-at-arms – cardboard helmet, broad-edged wooden sword, a plastic shield from the toyshop and a grubby white night-gown. The boy was unmistakably a Moor, with a floppy towel-turban precariously wound around his head, and a robe apparently stitched together of old dusters. I asked each of them, as a matter of form, whom they represented. 'I am the Christian *caballero,*' said the girl brightly, hitching her helmet up. The boy, however, had more sense of history. '*I am the others!*' he darkly replied, and bent his scimitar between his hands.

Cádiz Cathedral

Nor were the Moors the only Orientals to bring a tang or a smoulder to Spain – itself a country, for all its brackish magnificence, that sometimes seems short of salt. It is almost five hundred years since the Jews were expelled from Spain, but even now you often feel their presence – shadowy, muted, but pervasive still.

Their position in Spanish society, before their expulsion (or conversion) in 1492, fluctuated from ignominy to near-supremacy. The Visigoths often treated them abominably – under King Erwig, for instance, their hair was cropped, their property was confiscated, their evidence was not acceptable in a court of law, and they were given a year to recant their faith. Under the Muslims, on the other hand, they thrived – it was partly Jewish help that enabled the Moors to occupy Spain so swiftly. Beneath the tolerant aegis of Islam, for three centuries they

enjoyed their golden age: rich, honoured, cultivated, influential. There were towns in Spain that were entirely Jewish, and even Granada was known as the City of Jews. The Jews were the doctors of Moorish Spain, the philosophers, occasionally the diplomats, sometimes even the generals. Their own culture flourished as it seldom has in Europe, first in Granada, then in Toledo, and a reputation of almost Satanic ability surrounded their affairs. 'Priests go to Paris for their studies,' it used to be said, 'lawyers to Bologna, doctors to Salerno, and *devils to Toledo!*'

In the Christian kingdoms, before the completion of the Reconquest, the Jews intermittently prospered too, and at least among the ruling classes there was nothing pejorative to a Hebrew name. Alfonso VIII of Castile had a Jewish mistress, Pedro I of Aragón had a Jewish treasurer, in the synagogue called El Tránsito in Toledo an inscription on the wall honours, all in one whirl, the God of Israel, King Pedro the Cruel of Castile, and Samuel Levi. There were several Jewish Bishops of Burgos. It was only in the late fourteenth century, when the Reconquest was nearly complete, that the persecutions began again – and even then those Jews who accepted Christianity at first suffered no hardship, and formed indeed almost the whole merchant and banking class. The secret practice of Judaism, however, turned the people against them, and in the end the most devoutly Christian Jew was likely to be suspected of continuing his dreadful practices in private, burning Catholic babies when nobody was looking, or interspersing his Masses with black magic. The afternoon of the Spanish Jews burst into a blood-red sunset. Harassed by the Inquisition, deserted by their patron-kings, burnt in their hundreds, in the very year of the fall of Granada they were expelled *en masse* from Spanish soil. Thus the Catholic Monarchs, at the moment of Spain's greatest opportunity, threw out of their domains several hundred thousand of their most talented, efficient and necessary subjects.

They went without their possessions – capital they could take out, through letters of credit on banks owned by Jews elsewhere, but their libraries, their treasures, their land and their fine houses they left behind. They left their shades in the old Jewish quarters of the cities, from the hill-top ghetto of Toledo to the lovely labyrinth called Santa

Cruz in Seville. They left synagogues here and there, converted nowadays into churches
or museums, with crumbling friezes
of Hebrew script around their
walls, and dim memories of great
wealth. They left some hints of their
extraordinary talents. It is said that
the tremendous sculptor Gil de
Siloé was a Jew. Some people think
Columbus was – in his will he left
'half a mark of silver to a Jew who
used to live at the gate of the Jewry
in Lisbon'. St. Theresa had Jewish
origins. There was indeed a time
when most men of culture in Spain
were Jewish, and such a hegemony
cannot easily be expunged; the
Jews have left behind them a strain
of blood, a look in the eye, that is
apparent everywhere in the cities
of Spain, and subtly contributes
to her grandeur.

For several centuries after the
expulsion there were no Jews in
Spain at all, except those who had merged undetectably
into the Christian whole. They were remembered with dis-
taste. The palace called the Casa de los Picos in Segovia, which
is studded all over with diamond-shaped stones, is said to have
been faced in this way, after the expulsion, to blot out memories
of its former Jewish ownership: till then it had been known as the
House of the Jew, now it was the House of Bumps. In many a Spanish
cathedral you will find memorials to Christians allegedly murdered by
Jewish fanatics, and even today one guide to Seville describes a particular corner of the city as having been 'a last outpost of bearded Jews,
charlatans, and other queer characters'. A few Jews have come back,

Santa Cruz,
Seville

110

all the same. Some returned in the nineteenth century, and some have more recently arrived as refugees from Muslim Morocco. The English cemetery at Málaga is mostly occupied by people like John Mauger, Master of the Schooner *Lady Marsella*, Henry Hutting of the Brig *Dasher*, or William P. Beecher, of New Haven, Connecticut, whose tomb, erected to 'commemorate the merits of his useful life', is embellished with a mourning figure of Liberty and the thirteen stars of the original Union; tucked away in one corner, though, there is the grave of a solitary Jew, who died in 1961 of the Christian era, or 5,721 years after the Creation.

I once hailed a taxi in Madrid and asked the driver to take me to the synagogue. He was only faintly surprised by the commission, and after a few fruitless drives up drab back streets, knocking at closed doors and looking for mistaken street numbers, he deposited me at the door of a biggish modern office block. There, said he, were the Hebrews. Sure enough, when I had gone inside, and taken the elevator upstairs, and entered a small, dark, carpeted apartment, there the Hebrews were – small quiet men from North Africa, with the voice of a cantor giving a singing lesson in the room next door, and along the hall a plain, discreet little place of worship. They had no complaints, they said. The Government treated them kindly enough. They had not lately been accused of eating Christian infants, and if anyone thought them capable of sorcery, nobody had yet engaged their services.

In this they differed from their cousins, the Spanish gypsies, whose talents are always in demand. The most famous gypsies in the whole world are the painted dancers of the Sacromonte in Granada, a clan of prosperous, grasping, and exceedingly talented performers who batten upon the poor visitor with steely talons, plump him gasping upon a kitchen chair in a cave, offer him a glass of unspeakable wine, treat him to half an hour of the best folk-dancing in Europe, grossly overcharge him, and send him back to his hotel feeling rather as the yokels of folk-lore used to feel, when the devil had kept them up in a trance, footing it around a fairy ring all night. The zing, the flair, the unutterable nerve of the Sacromonte gypsies, which have made their name a swear-word wherever tourists gather to swop experiences, are characteristic of the Spanish *gitanos* – much the most exciting of all the aliens of Spain.

There are gypsies all over this country, pure or half-caste, raggety with their dogs and wagons on the lanes of Navarre, inexcusably swaggering through the streets of Granada, where they have been settled at least since the fifteenth century. One contemporary authority, Jean-Paul Clébert, says that in Spain they have 'found one of their most favourable homes', but it was not always so. Their life in Spain has been full of ups and downs. The Catholic Monarchs threatened to banish them, unless they gave up their gypsy life. Philip II tried to settle them in towns. Philip IV ordered that 'they be taken from their places of habitation, separated from one another, with express prohibition to come together publicly or in secret'. Charles II forbade them to own horses. Charles III called them Neo-Castilians, and gave their horses back again. The prophets of the French romantic movement seized upon their dances, their costumes, their rhythms, and their strident voices and made them synonymous, to the world at large, with the reputation of Spain herself. Much that seems to us most Spanish is really gypsy. Bull-fighting is an art in which the *gitanos* have always excelled; flamenco they have made their own; wherever a castanet clicks in Spain, a heel taps, a pair of hands claps, or a deep sad voice wails through the night, then the influence of the gypsies is somewhere about.

Granada

Ubeda

They possess, to a degree no other Spaniard does, a gift for irrepressible enthusiasm. They crackle. In the delightful little Andalusian town of Ubeda I was approached one night by two gypsies who asked if I would like to hear their companion, an older man of distinctly theatrical appearance, sing the *cante jondo*. He was, they said, a most distinguished performer, well known in all the best caves of the Sacromonte – which is to say, in the *gitano* context, top of the bill at the Palladium. The singer's throat was muffled in an elegant spotted scarf, rather in the Barrymore tradition, and he complained, with an anxious arpeggio or two, of a sore throat. He agreed to do his best, though, and off we set towards a nearby café. It was rather like joining a trio of flamboyant picaresque rogues in a minor bank robbery. The place was full of solemn townsmen, playing earnest games of dominoes, who looked up as we entered, in a flurry of badinage and conceit, rather as though we were interrupting the sermon. We were, however, unperturbed. Up the steps we went, now and then breaking into a few clattering dance steps, and clearing ourselves a place at a trestle table, and ordering wine all around, we sat down, gave that lofty tenor a few respectful moments of silence, and presently burst into song.

Never in my whole life have I had more fun, or been more stimulated by animal high spirits. The great man, breaking his melancholy, soon led us from the sad *cante jondo* into the most raucous kind of flamenco, and before long that whole room was an uproar of violent clapping, clicked fingers, wild laughs and cries, stamped feet, ear-splitting songs and side-splitting witticisms. The domino-players abandoned their games, the floorboards shook, and presently the proprietor, shouldering his way through the din, interrupted to say that if we wished to continue the entertainment, we must do so elsewhere. So we parted, Barrymore, his two merry agents, and I, only pausing in the moonlight for a last actor-managerial clearing of the throat and a brief altercation about performing fees – those splendid fellows at first demanding, not with much conviction, rather more than five times what they actually got.

Ah, the gypsies! If they are not the salt of Spain, they are the spiciest of sauces.

Many another foreigner has left his mark. The Roman has left his great aqueducts and fortifications, the theatres of Mérida and Sagunto, the villas of Tarragona, the city wall that surrounds the cathedral city of Lugo, or the noble bridge across the Tagus at Alcántara – a name which means, indeed, merely The Bridge. The Spanish bull-ring is

The Roman amphitheatre, Sagunto

clearly descended from the Roman amphitheatre – if you have doubts, look at the ruined ring at Alcoy, north of Alicante, which was wrecked during the Civil War, and now looks exactly like an archaeological specimen in Rome. Roman place names are all over Spain – Badajoz means Pax Augusta, Saragossa comes from Caesarea Augusta. Olives from Roman stock are still the best. Some people think that *gazpacho* is really the Roman *posca*, a standard Roman Army ration; and some travellers consider that the most evocative memorial in all Spain is the unfinished Roman obelisk that stands in the shade of a wild garden north of Tarragona, dappled by sunshine, fragrant with pines, with the sweet breezes of the Mediterranean ruffling its cypresses, and a strong emanation of dryads.

French influence in Spain has been persistent and profound. French monks of Cluny created the Santiago pilgrimage. French architects inspired half the great cathedrals. A Frenchman was first Archbishop of Toledo. Thirty-four expeditions came from France to help the Spanish Christians in their crusades against the Moors. Throughout modern Spanish history, France has been Spain's symbol of modernism – sometimes feared, often detested, frequently envied, but never quite out of the Spanish mind. Dutchmen too, Germans, Flemings, and Italians have all brought their skills to Spain, and left behind a curtain-wall, a tapestry, the slope of a buttress or the angle of a pediment. The telephone system still bears the stamp of the Americans who used to manage it, and who stuck to their switchboards with such tenacity that throughout the Civil War they served both sides impartially – often the first news of a city's loss reached the Government when some Minister telephoned the local commander from Madrid, to be answered by the enemy. Foreign capital from many countries has been essential to the jerky development of Spanish industry. The Army, with its jackboots, goosesteps, Africa Korps caps and Nazi steel helmets, is a reminder that foreign troops were fighting on this soil less than forty years ago: sometimes, on the lonely steppe, you will find a small memorial, in the old German script, to some young pilot of the Condor Legion, and outside Salamanca there is an ironically beautiful memorial to all the Italians who died in these parts for the gimcrack cause of Fascism.

And, of course, you cannot escape the British, the sea-gyp-sies, whose history touches the story of Spain so often and so intimately that John of Gaunt had a perfectly reasonable claim to the throne of Castile, Charles I of England once came to Madrid, dashingly incognito, to find himself a Spanish bride, and the Dukes of Wellington are, to this day, Dukes of Ciudad Rodrigo too. The British flag still flies over Gibraltar, and there is a large British colony in Spain proper – thousands of expatriates have escaped from the drizzle and the taxation to Andalusia or the Balearics. There are many Spanish Anglophiles: Jerez, whose sherry sells in vast quantities on the English market, and whose industry was partly built by Englishmen, is recognizably British still, full of impeccable Anglo-Spanish accents, handsome hacking jackets and visiting gentry from the London office. And most telling of all the figures of the relationship, perhaps, are the British old-age pensioners who, finding winter life on the Costa del Sol both cheaper and more fun than retirement at home, come out in their rollicking groups each year to occupy the grateful holiday hotels: for very soon, often enough, these old dears succumb to the environment, are transformed into honorary Andalusians themselves, and are to be seen in the middle of the morning happily flirting with total strangers over wine glasses beside the sea.

Jerez de la frontera

116

6 WILD SPAIN

El Rocío

Where the Guadalquivir River comes down to the sea, the upperworks of the ships from Seville riding queerly through the palms and sandbanks, there lies a great marshland, the Coto Doñana – the biggest roadless area in western Europe. The best way to sample this extraordinary region of marsh and sand dune – short of taking a string of mules and making for the middle of it – is to visit a fascinating village called El Rocío, twenty-odd miles off the road from Seville to Huelva.

It is chiefly a place of pilgrimage, for its imposing modern church contains a miraculous figure of the Virgin whose annual fiesta is one of the most colourful events in the Spanish calendar. Half the buildings of the village are white shrines, chapels, hermitages or pilgrims' hostels: the rest are simple single-storey cottages, and among them there runs a series of wide green swards, shaded by big cork trees. Most of the houses are modern, the village now doubling as pious destination and holiday resort, but the place still possesses a quality of mystery and remoteness: and if this is partly because of the Virgin's presence there, it is partly because El Rocío stands on the very edge of the Coto Doñana. If you wander down beyond the houses, following the sound of children's voices, there you will see, beyond the muddy shallows where the small boys play, the swamps, reeds and sand dunes of the great nature reserve stretching away towards the sea.

It looks illimitable and almost impenetrable, so thick are its high rushes, so flat, hot, and hazy its horizon. Scarcely a sign of life disturbs it, not a rustle in the rushes, not the smoke of a distant steamer – only an occasional gliding bird, perhaps, or a croak out of the sun. It is, though, one of the richest wildlife refuges in Europe, and teems with birds, mammals, and multifarious insects. Here all the resources of pristine Spain are left unsnared, unshot, and uneaten (except for the predations of a few enterprising poachers, who concentrate on herons' eggs). There are lynxes on the Coto Doñana, and wild boars, mongooses, chameleons, sand skinks, snakes of a dozen varieties, tortoises and terrapins, wildcats, genets, flamingoes, great crested grebes, glossy ibises, spoonbills, bee-eaters, golden orioles, tarantulas, scorpions, Algerian Owls and Edible Dormice. Its midges are so numerous that their mating swarms rise above the marshland like thick black columns of smoke. Its birds are so varied that in one recent afternoon, in an area of about a hundred acres, a single ornithologist spotted 1,891 birds of 35 species. It even boasts the only wild camels in Europe, remnants of a troop which were brought to Spain from the Canary Islands in 1829, and proved such abysmal failures with pack or plough that they were turned loose into the Coto; by the early 1960s there were only three animals left, but they were reinforced by dromedaries left over from the filming in Spain of *Lawrence of Arabia*, and can now occasionally be seen splashing eerily through the marshes in clouds of salt spray.

All this in Andalusia, a morning's drive from Seville, in the second half of the twentieth century! But the Coto Doñana is only a climax, for Spain as a whole remains the wildest country of western Europe, except perhaps the northernmost part of Scandinavia. The human population of Spain has risen from some eighteen million at the beginning of the century to some thirty million today. The people are mostly packed, however, into a few densely populated areas, and are pressing ever more insistently out of the country into the towns. At least a third of the Spaniards live in the seven biggest cities of the country, and even in rural areas, except in the north-west, they are grouped in tight hubs of population. It is thought that Spain can support double her present population, if the land is worked properly, but even then half her country will be uncultivated. Even in the arable areas, there is plenty of room for wildness; and beyond the fields there always rise the vast, spare, rock-ribbed mountains, which can never be spoilt or tamed. As recently as the twenties there were fullscale expeditions into the Sierra Nevada, and there were some high corners of the Picos de Europa, in Asturias, that were unexplored until the 1960s.

There are bears still in Spain, in the gloomy mountains of the north. There are wolves in some parts: on a blistered beach in Murcia I once found a wolf-corpse, half eaten by ants and grinning maliciously. There are great bustards, most imposing of game birds, all over Andalusia: huge pompous creatures, with muscular necks and bristly moustaches, whose great wing-beat is one of the most tremendous sounds of ornithology. The fighting bulls of Spain, bred deliberately to ferocity,

A landscape in the Pyrenees

are a far cry from the test-tube hybrids of less elemental countries: powerful, thick-set, and heavy-chested, they roam the great bull-pastures like proper monsters, and are only rounded up with respect, by lithe experienced gauchos with lances. Spain is a great place for owls, gazing disapprovingly at the passer-by from telegraph wire or umbrella pine: Spanish legend says that an owl sat upon the cross-beam of the Cross, and that ever since its descendants have been hooting *'Cruz! Cruz!'*. Spain is full of mole-crickets, shrill little underground insects whose goggle eyes you may sometimes see peering sleeplessly out of their burrows, and whose buzz is so energetic that their whole bodies vibrate down there like the radiators of very old motor-cars.

Cáceres

Eagles and vultures swoop around many a Spanish cliff-face. Fastidious egrets stalk the water-meadows of the west. Gay little crested hoopoes glide enchantingly across every province. Frogs croak so loud that they sound like puppy-dogs in the dark. Seagulls go as far inland as the salt marshes of La Mancha, and swarms of martins give to many Spanish castles the 'delicate air' that Banquo liked. The nightingales of the Generalife gardens, above Granada, tirelessly live up to their reputation as they sing away among the cypresses. Snakes wriggle perpetually across the lanes of Spain, glow-worms flicker in the night, lizards bask at every picnic site, flying beetles, giant moths and unexpectedly vicious bees are constantly hurling themselves at your windscreen or easing themselves through your bedroom window. All over this country you may pay your respects to the solemn chapter of Spanish storks, clicking their gullets on church-towers and chimney-pots from Navarre to Andalusia. Their capital is the Estremaduran city of Cáceres, whose mediaeval houses and cluttered hillside streets seem to cower beneath the domination of the storks' nests; but they are at their most lordly upon the Roman aqueduct at Mérida, through whose arches the big trains steam towards Portugal, and upon whose highest stones the great storks sit in majesty.

It was in Spain that Charles I of England was given trout, out of the Segovia hill streams, so big that he actually took the trouble to write home about them – 'certaine troute of extraordinary greatnesse'. Throughout the mountain masses of Spain delectable unfrequented trout streams abound, and the fjord-like estuaries of the north-west are full of salmon. Nothing is better organized, in the whole gamut of Spanish life, than the system by which the fish of the Atlantic and Mediterranean coasts are hurtled across Spain to the capital: a tragic sense of urgency informs the process, from the swift silent loading of the ice-boxes at Valencia or San Sebastián to the pounding of the big trucks through the night – ensuring that whatever else may happen in the world, whatever strikes or outrages may mortify Spain, still there will be red mullet, lobster, oysters, and spider-crabs for lunch in Madrid tomorrow. There are always fish about in Spain: fish in

A fishing village

the stream beside the road, fish glistening in the huge markets, dried fillets of fish in boxes on grocers' counters, trapped fish leaping helplessly in the salt-pans of Cádiz, fish brought by mule or truck to the remotest mountain village, or – if they count as fish – those little wisps of elvers, hardly old enough to be animate, which are offered to you like dishes of some fine-spun *pasta* in every Valencian eating-house.

Behind the wild fauna, too, peering wistfully over lynx and mongoose, armies of domesticated animals keep Spain close to nature. This is a country still visibly impelled by muscle-power. The tractors and the cars are now ubiquitous, but four stout legs and a good wind are still perfectly normal prerequisites of Spanish locomotion. It is a country of horses, from the pampered beauties of the Seville Feria to the tired Rosinantes which, looking much too tall for their duties, still labour around the Spanish cities with their hackney-carriages. Spain and horses have always gone together, and Spanish stud mares have always been in demand – among the ancients, not least for their supposed powers of virgin birth, what Sir Thomas Browne mockingly described as 'sub-ventaneous conception from the Western Wind'. Spaniards love and understand horses, and even the most fanatical of bull-fight *aficionados* will sometimes admit to a pang of sympathy for the picadors' wretched mounts (whose vocal cords are cut to stop them screaming).

The brawny Spanish mule, though retreating before the rumble of modernism, handsomely holds his own. The Spanish goat still prospers: in many a little Spanish town you may see a herd trotted around from door to door, to allow the owner of each animal to pop her inside for a minute or two, milk her, and return her to the care of the goatherd. Oxen still haul the haywains (though no longer the ploughshares) of the north. No sight is more instantly Spanish than the flocks of thin sheep which, guarded by a single tongue-tied shepherd boy, roam the bare tablelands, and for thousands of sentimental travellers the most beguiling figure in all Spain is that paragon of pretty patience, the donkey.

Dogs are rather eccentric in Spain. Some look like scented lapdogs but do the dirty work on farms. Some ride precariously on the backs of donkeys, like Venetian dogs on the prows of market-barges. Some wear long thin sticks beneath their chins, to prevent them from scavenging. Some are apparently of independent means, and are often to be encountered in lonely places, huge spiked collars around their necks, giving you only a cursory glance of inspection as they pace thoughtfully off towards their next appointment. Very few are unfriendly. The Spaniard is popularly supposed to be cruel to animals, and to vagabonds he often is; but to his own beast he is nearly always courteous – his big mongrel dog fears no whip and snarls at no stranger, his docile ass has an affectionate nickname, his lovely Andalusian mare trots among the orange blossoms in a glow of pride and friendship. In Spanish the pronoun *tú* is reserved for relatives, intimates, and animals. Charles I of Spain so loved his cat and his parrot that after his death in the monastery of Yuste they were sent all the way to Valladolid in the royal sedan chair; the Cid so loved his mare Babieca that her burial place is still marked, outside the convent of San Pedro de Cardeña, near Burgos; the sixteenth-century tomb of Bishop Villalan in Almería Cathedral has a loyal terrier at its feet; I once saw some workmen, doing a job of work in the Alhambra, taking a parrot along with them in a cage.

It is perfectly true that a century ago working people in Bilbao used to eat cats, stewed in sherry; on the other hand there is no more affectionate piece of sculpture in Spain than the famous column-head

The monastery, Yuste

Tarragona Cathedral

in Tarragona Cathedral which portrays a big tomcat, taken joyously to his funeral by a company of rats, suddenly coming to life and eating them all. The open-air pet stalls in the Ramblas at Barcelona, where you may buy anything from a mouse to a monkey, are always surrounded by doting bystanders, and the cat who lives in the grille outside the south door of Valencia Cathedral is, as you may see from the hideous mess of fish-bones and gristle that lines his lair, never without his well-wishers. To the Spaniard the animal is part of the universal pattern: if a vagrant cat is stoned, or a whining pye-dog kicked away, it is because they have acquired no place in the pyramid of being, and have no right to approach it. Dignity springs from order, and order admits no strays.

There is something soothing to this sense of natural decorum, just as the pristine landscapes of Spain can often calm the anxious nerves. Behind all the plodding, fluttering, thundering, or wriggling menagerie of Spain, there stands always the sweet silence and emptiness of the Spanish land, daubed in spring with unbelievable blues, reds, and yellows of wild flowers, and still preserving the innocence of a virgin soil. Spain smells of nature: rosemary, thyme, lavender, the homely smell of wood fires, the chemical smell of pine woods after rain, the blowzy smell of orange blossom and roses, the heady smell of a million wild flowers – of the ten thousand varieties of flowers known in Europe, more than half are found in Spain. The Western world offers few pleasures more intoxicating than the delight of awaking, early one spring morning, in a tent upon a Spanish hillside, and looking out through the flap, as the sausages sizzle upon the cooker, across the wide sierra. Perhaps you may see the distant campanile of a village, or hear the faint mellow clanging of its bell. Perhaps, far down in the valley, a solitary muleteer is labouring to market, his head shrouded in a brown blanket. Up on that hill, though, you are all on your own. A kite keeps an eye on you overhead. A party of speckled pigs, high on the slope above, snorts around the bluebells. As the sun warms up there is a buzzing, a humming, a whizzing of small insects in the air, a hooting and chuckling of birds, a chafing of crickets in the grass. The morning is scented with damp turf, blossoms, tent canvas and sausages. By the time you reach the marmalade, you feel you could walk a hundred miles that day, swim the Channel before lunch, or take on single-handed the entire personnel of the Inland Revenue.

For there never was a country where landscape more evidently moulded character. If a sweet spring morning with sausages can do this to you, imagine how your personality would be affected by a lifetime of harsh living on the fierce plateau. The wildness of this country has undoubtedly made the Spaniards a more ferocious people than most. The 'Spanish fury', which Livy detected and named, was generally latent for forty years after the Civil War; but hardly had Franco died, and the strong arm of his discipline been relaxed, than political terrorism erupted in the Basque country and Catalonia, and the old spectres walked again. Spain's savage reputation dies hard, and rightly so. A century ago an encounter with bandits, preferably bloodless, was a *sine qua non* of a really satisfactory Spanish tour, and even in the 1960s, though the last desperate outlaws of the Republic had been

The castle, Coca, Old Castile

winkled out from their Pyrenean hideouts ten years before – even then people would still take you by the arm, when you proposed to go wandering in Spain, and warn you to be careful.

I suppose the *legenda negra* of Spain – the 'black legend' that sensitive Spaniards are so anxious to refute – was born with the conquistadores, whose rule in South America was sometimes wise and generous, but whose methods of imposing it were often barbaric. What more ferocious stories are there in history than the chronicles of Cortés in Mexico, or Pizarro in Peru – tremendous tales of daring and ebullience, which nearly always start with a pious intent, and nearly always end in murder? The Spanish soldier of the golden age, striding through Europe in lace jabot and topboots, seemed to himself the very personification of Christian chivalry; but the image of *The Lances* was not the world's vision of the Spanish temperament. Still less did Torquemada's own conception of the Spanish Inquisition – a prophylactic of the public conscience – correspond to the impression it made upon people abroad. The horrors of torture, public recantation, degradation and death by fire horribly impressed the sensibilities of Europe: for though they were not uniquely Spanish, in Spain they were, like most things, carried to belated extremes – the Inquisition rose to power in Spain at a time when, in other countries, it was already waning. Many thousands of Jews, Moors, Protestants, and miscellaneous heretics were executed by the Inquisition; once they had been named, and had undergone the fearful ceremony of the *auto-da-fé* (when they filed before the public dressed grotesquely in yellow sacking and fools' caps), nothing could save them: off they went on donkey-back to be burnt, and if they repented at the last moment, the only privilege the Church allowed them was the mercy of strangulation.

And if, during the long centuries of obscurity, this memory of Spain was beginning to blur, and incompetent military upstarts replaced the dreadful cardinals as symbols of Spanish authority – if the black legend seemed to be fading at last, the horrors of the Civil War revived it with a vengeance. Never was a conflict fought more bitterly. Almost every page of its history reeks with cruelty. Sometimes it is the Army of Africa, Franco's spearhead, whose ghastly revenges still oppress us, as we read of the blood running down the streets of Toledo, or the hundreds of unarmed men slaughtered in the bull-ring of Badajoz. Sometimes it is the frenzied militiamen of the Republican armies, crucifying priests, castrating landowners, cutting off women's breasts or humiliating nuns. Nobody, it seems, was immune to the infection. At one end the mob often tore its victims limb from limb. At the other the secret courts of the Communists condemned their prisoners first, and tortured them later. The thirst for blood, the taste for violence, the opportunity for vengeance, the savagery of despair or resentment – all these passions seized the nation then, and make its ordinary people, seen

Crosses near Segovia

in the records of the history books, seem as terrible in their instincts as any mediaeval master of the rack.

Is this something peculiar to the Spanish? Is it some ghoulish yearning for blood, or some ironic by-product of superior sensibilities? Eye-witnesses assure us that even the worst butcheries of the Civil War were generally committed not by sadists or thugs, but by men who really thought they were pursuing an honourable purpose. Certainly the Spaniard does cherish a particular view towards death itself. The death of the bull is the Moment of Truth; the death of a man is the climax of life – an unwanted climax, to be sure, but something that expresses a kind of fulfilment for a people unfulfilled in history and environment (for the spare grandeur of the Spanish tableland does have a sapless or sterile air). The Spanish village cemetery stands well away from the houses, like a full stop, and the brooding presence of death has always been a Spanish preoccupation. Beneath the magnificent tombs of the Catholic Monarchs, in Granada Cathedral, their plain lead coffins lie in an unornamented crypt, a dry *memento mori* to every sightseer. When Alfonso XIII sailed away into exile on a Spanish cruiser, in 1931, he took the ship's ensign with him when he disembarked, to serve as his shroud when the time came. In the exquisite hermitages above Córdoba there are preserved two skulls which formed the gloomy crockery of a distinguished hermit of the past, the Marqués of Santaella and Villaverde; from one that world-weary nobleman drank his water, from the other he ate his bread. Nor is the death-taste dying, even now. When I once paid a visit to the Spanish Minister of Information, in Madrid, he gave me as an official souvenir of my visit Manuel Sánches Camargo's monumental *Death and Spanish Painting*, with 193 funereal plates, and line illustrations of skeletons in the text.

What is macabre to us is often beautiful to the Spaniard, so that congealed blood is a favourite component of Spanish religious portraiture, and the holy relics of Spanish religion are often sickeningly close to dissection ward or abattoir. A characteristic miraculous recovery was that of little Don Carlos, heir to Philip II, who was cured of his wasting disease by the corpse of a monk called Fray Diego, dug up from its tomb and laid beside him on the sick-bed (though the poor boy was

The Royal Palace, Madrid

always mis-shapen, as you may see from his asymmetrical suit of armour in the Royal Palace at Madrid). To the Spaniard there is evidently no physical repulsion in death. He is not generally a man of much imagination, he is not often a coward, and it is, I suppose, difficult to feel quite so guilty about a murder when you know that your victim is only enjoying his Moment of Truth at last.

Nobody can be kinder than the Spaniard, with his overriding love of children, his lack of envy, his guileless courtesy. The Spanish crime rate today is still among the lowest in Europe, and there is probably no country, outside Hunza or the Sherpa provinces, where the visitor can feel so generally certain that the change will be correct and the price honest. Spain is often an irritating country, but rarely seems spiteful: even traffic accidents, for all the world's conception of Spanish volatility, do not usually degenerate into violent tempers.

Even so, it is less than half a century since the blood ran down the Spanish gutters, since this very same kindly people murdered one another, burnt its own churches, martyred its own priests, slaughtered many an inoffensive woman, and proved that the Spanish fury was still a fact of life. Perhaps violence goes with simplicity. If so, Spain will harbour her reputation for many a long year yet, for as long as the mules pace her mountain tracks and the Algerian Owl looks down, all goggle-eyes and hauteur, upon the Edible Dormouse.

7
THE
SOLDIERS

Véleg Blanco, Castile

War is a vocation of the Spaniards. They have lately enjoyed a long period of peace, but this is a rarity in their history, which is punctuated always by conflict. Their country is a castle, moated and ramparted, and inside it citadels are everywhere, giving it all a military air. There are resplendent castles on hilltops, like the shimmer of Vélez Blanco in Andalusia, part of whose inside was ripped out in 1903, and shipped to New York. There are Christmas-cake castles, all turrets and drawbridges, like the ineffable Coca near Segovia — every boy's idea of a proper fortress. There are museum-castles, like Belmonte, south of Cuenca, whose janitor will wave you good-bye all the way down the long ramp of the fosse, only interrupting himself to consult his great gold watch to see if it is nearly closing time. There are trim private castles perched on humps, and there are sprawling Moorish castles, supervising white cities of the south, or peering rheumily down strategic valleys. There are castles that are still castles, with guns protruding from their loopholes, and frowning soldiers in their sentry-boxes. There are castles that are hotels, like the splendid fortress of Ciudad Rodrigo, near the Portuguese frontier. There are castles that are villages, like the quaint stronghold of Guadalest, near Benidorm, whose walls are full of houses, whose keep is the cemetery, and whose church belfry stands so high upon the ramparts that a long rope is left trailing down to the alley below, for the convenience of the bell-ringer.

There are castles that are university departments, like the picture-postcard fortress of Peñíscola, on the Valencian coast, which has been beautifully done up with plate glass and panelling, and is garrisoned by foreign students. There are impeccable round castles like the one above Palma, in Majorca; there are shapeless crumbled castles, like old decayed teeth in the hills; there are castles so grand that the whole world knows them, like the Alhambra, and castles so unassuming that you have to look hard down back streets before you find them at all. The castles of Spain are lieutenants to her cathedrals. Castile itself is called after them, and their name has gone into half the languages of Europe: a castle in Spain is what the ambitious Crusader dreamt of, when he fastened his greaves to go to war.

They remind us that Spain was forged in battle. Her castles were frontier fortresses, pushed southwards century by century as the Moors were expelled, and the Spanish kings moved their capitals from front to front. Civil war has been a commonplace of Spanish history, and there are not many Spanish cities that do not boast of some heroic episode in the past, or cannot flaunt some warlike royal motto:

*The Castle,
Peñíscola, Valencia*

135

Very Noble (says Seville's, for instance), *Very Loyal, Very Heroic and Invincible*. Scarcely a corner of Spain has not been a battlefield, at one time or another, and Spanish soldiers served not only on Hadrian's Wall, against the barbarians, but also with the Nazis in Russia, against the atheists. 'Back to the struggle,' wrote Byron of the Spaniards, 'baffled in the strife, War, war is still the cry, *War even to the knife!*'

Even now Spain seems a country of soldiers, military in a kind that is almost obsolete elsewhere in the Western world. There are jet aircraft in Spain, of course, and American naval bases, and spanking little radar domes, perched upon high vantage-points, that are part of the Western defence system. The Spanish armed forces, though, both in their manner and their vast numbers, seem to spring from the huge conscript armies of yesterday, as though nuclear bombs have not yet entered the Spanish strategic assessments, and battleships are still the thing. All the scenes of old-fashioned military life, such as are portrayed in nineteenth-century Russian paintings, can be seen in the flesh in Spain. Here are the reluctant conscripts, shouldering their first kit-bags, parading raggedly in the town square to a shouting of sergeants and the sniffing of a few disconsolate mothers. Here are the generals, leaving their swanky hotels in a cloud of flags, aides-de-camp, bowing managers and befurred women. Here you may see the draft on the railway station, waiting for a connection that is two hours late, their caps tilted over their eyes, their feet propped up in heavy boots, on their faces an expression of glazed fatalism, in their hands a pack of dirty cards. Here a parade comes down the road, bound for an exercise or an inspection, led by an equestrian colonel with drawn sword, and marching as though death or glory really were the immediate alternatives. The officer of Spain is still a proud and gaudy figure, even if he is sometimes to be seen, after duty, chugging off on a motorbike to his afternoon job at the bank. The ships of Spain still put out to sea in a fine flurry of ensigns, trumpet calls, and traditional goings-on. The troops who man the northern bastions, like Jaca in Navarre, or Seo de Urgel below the pass from Andorra, stand to their guns in postures so theatrically watchful that you might suppose the legions of France had already packed their palliasses to cross the Pyrenees. Outside a barracks in Avila I once saw a soldier, in a superb cameo of old-

The monastery
of Santa Cruz de los
Seros
Jaca, Huesca

school military custom,
actually place his bugle
bell-down upon the ground
in order to water the
orderly-room flower-bed.

It is easy to laugh – the
Spaniards were withdrawn
from the world so long that in
many ways they have a Victorian look.
The Spanish forces may seem archaic, but
nobody has recently doubted their ability to fight,
and in Spain the profession of arms commands a special kind of
esteem. Cervantes was a soldier, and so was St. Ignatius, who
organized his Jesuits on rigidly military lines. St. Theresa wished she
could go to war. Velázquez loved the military aesthetic. The poet
Alonso de Ercilla y Zúñiga wrote some of his best lyrics on his saddle-
pommel, the poet Jorge Manrique was killed during the storming of a
Moorish castle in La Mancha, the poet Garcilaso de la Vega died while
assaulting a stronghold in France. Lope de Vega wrote eleven

thousand lines of epic verse while at sea with the Spanish Armada. Calderón the dramatist was granted a pension for gallantry in action against Catalan rebels. In Spain St. James is honoured first as the soldier he never was, and only secondly as the missionary he wasn't either. This is a soldier's country through and through, and if ever the flags ceased to fly above those castles, or even the orderly-room flowers to blossom beneath the watering can, Spain would be Spain no more.

It was war of the most swashbuckling kind that gave her that one moment of supremacy, early in the sixteenth century, ushering her once and for all into the ranks of the great nations. It was not really her first experience of a New World: the Reconquest itself had been a pioneering process, as immense empty territories were captured and settled with Christian colonists from the north. The Spanish exploit in the Americas, however, was one of the most astonishing adventures in the whole history of mankind, and brilliantly demonstrated the martial genius of this people.

If you travel north-eastwards from the Coto Doñana, across the Sierra Morena and the wastelands of Estremadura, you will presently come to the town of Trujillo, where the conquistador Pizarro was born. It greets you with some rotted ramparts, and to reach its central plaza you must wind a cautious way through narrow overhung lanes, cramped, dark and shabby. At first it does not feel in the least imperial, but before very long the alley broadens, you pass between a pair of tottering mansions, the sun suddenly blazes in your eyes, and there before you in the wide square stands a statue of Francisco Pizarro. The moment when you see this thing, when you burst out of the shadow into the dazzling sunlight of the plaza, to find that old adventurer gigantic upon his horse, head up, beard jutting, and helmet-plumes astream – this sudden moment at Trujillo is, at least to my tastes, one of the supreme revelations of Spanish travel. It was Pizarro, you will remember, who overthrew the Incas in one of the most outrageously audacious campaigns ever undertaken – 183 men against an Empire! – who established Spanish authority in Peru, and who ruled the country

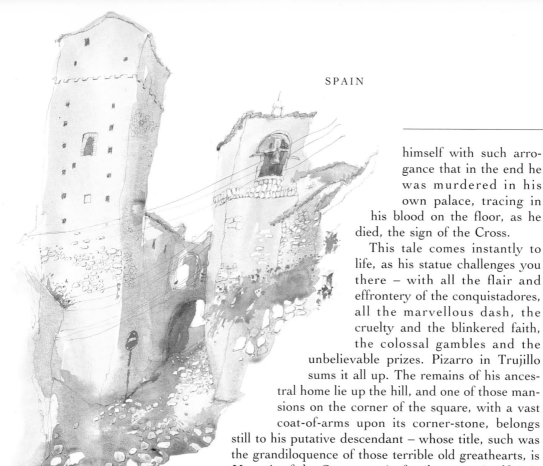

The home of
Pizarro, Trujillo

himself with such arrogance that in the end he was murdered in his own palace, tracing in his blood on the floor, as he died, the sign of the Cross.

This tale comes instantly to life, as his statue challenges you there – with all the flair and effrontery of the conquistadores, all the marvellous dash, the cruelty and the blinkered faith, the colossal gambles and the unbelievable prizes. Pizarro in Trujillo sums it all up. The remains of his ancestral home lie up the hill, and one of those mansions on the corner of the square, with a vast coat-of-arms upon its corner-stone, belongs still to his putative descendant – whose title, such was the grandiloquence of those terrible old greathearts, is Marquis of the Conquest. As for the statue itself, it is only proper that there should be a replica of it in the Plaza de los Reyes in Lima; and even more appropriate that, by a happy quirk of sculpture, the conquistador is brandishing a formidable sword, but is provided with no scabbard.

Estremadura was pre-eminently the country of the adventurers, for many of them went to the New World specifically to escape its deadening poverty and parochialism. Often they returned rich, and the region is full of their memorials, poignant reminders of Spain's brief dominion of the world. The old part of Cáceres, that city of the storks, is embellished everywhere with the heraldry of imperial *nouveaux-riches*, whose principal object of retirement seems to have been to bask in titled superiority to the family next door. Elsewhere in Spain, too, the empire-builders have left their crumbling mark. There is a small village in Aragón called Corella, which is scarcely visited by strangers from one year to the next, but which is strikingly redolent of imperial activities:

almost every big house boasts some memory of the New World – in this one was born a Governor of Peru, in that a famous general died – and half of them bear the escutcheons of families ennobled by the course of empire. Cuenca, that curious cliff-top city of Castile, has especially pungent memories of the conquistadores: most of its mansions, now sadly dingy, were built with American gold, and it was to this cold and froward city, whose most famous inhabitant was Torrealba the great wizard, that the last of the Aztec royal princes, Don Pedro, was brought to die.

Columbus was neither a Spaniard nor a conquistador, but he is naturally inescapable in Spain. You may see his great tomb in Seville Cathedral, the monastery of La Rábida where he completed his plans, the bridge near Granada where the messengers from the Catholic Monarchs caught him up, called him to the royal presence, and thus made the New World Spanish. In Barcelona, where they fondly like to claim that Columbus was born, they have erected a huge statue of him on a pillar above the quays, with a replica of the *Santa Maria* in the harbour at his feet. At Seville, a port which for many years held a royal monopoly of trade with the Americas, they preserve the remnants of his library, its books inscribed with his mysterious cipher. And some pungent suggestions of the great sailor linger at Palos de la Frontera, the little port in western Andalusia from which he sailed on his first Atlantic voyage. It is a port no longer, its harbour is filled in with green squashy meadows and bean fields, and an unfortunate memorial promenade has been built at the water's edge, extending with the statutory Spanish plethora of lamp-standards across the marshlands to the estuary. The village still proudly remembers, though, Columbus's fellow-captains, who were natives of this place; above the sea stands the stout old church, where a farewell Mass was said for the

Cuenca, Castile

141

crews; not quite obliterated by a new highway is the old Roman well where the little ships were watered; and always beyond the houses the Río Tinto flows away past Huelva to the open sea. It is a place of great character, one of the few places on either side of the ocean where the person of Christopher Columbus is recognizable not as a wraith or an enigma, but as a master-mariner.

Scratches on the stones of Spain – such are these mementos of the great adventure. Sometimes a name on a signpost – Valparaíso, perhaps, Buenos Aires, Las Vegas, or Los Alamos – reminds you how much the Spaniards gave to the new countries of the West. More often an echo or a hint will emphasize how little of permanence they brought back. Drinking chocolate, they say, was first tasted by Spaniards at Montezuma's court – nowadays they flavour it highly with cinnamon, brew it very thickly, and sip it with transcendent daintiness from tiny china cups. Some people say that the Spanish love of skulls, bones, and old blood was stimulated by the Aztecs, who had similar predilections. I like myself to fancy that contemporary Spanish architecture, which has a weakness for huge cliff-like structures, with small windows and monolithic façades, has been influenced by dim memories of the Pueblo Indians' square mud villages: certainly the dry-wall techniques of Majorca, stone blocks balanced with uncanny exactitude one upon another, are directly related in manner to the gargantuan masonry walls of the Incas. In the Escorial there is a bishop's mitre decorated with Aztec feathers. In Majorca there is a town called Inca. The park policemen of the Alhambra wear warm woolly ponchos, like Bolivian shepherds.

Here and there across Spain, too, there are reminders that *Hispanidad*,

The Basilica, Montserrat

142

The monastery, La Rábida,
near Palos de la frontera

the idea of a Spanishness common to Old World and New, does have some meaning. Most of the lamps in the Basilica of Montserrat, sent to replace those destroyed by Napoleon's soldiery, were given by faithful adherents of the cult in Peru, Mexico, and the Argentine. In the Sanctuary of the Great Promise at Valladolid, named for a pledge divinely given to a Jesuit priest in the eighteenth century – 'I will reign in Spain more than in any other part of the world' – there is a chapel presented by all the American republics which were once Spanish possessions, and in Columbus's monastery of La Rábida there are specimens, neatly packed in wooden boxes, of their separate soils. Students from Latin America still come to study at the Spanish universities. The elegant northern resort of San Sebastián owes some of its prosperity to the faithful attendance, season after season, of rich and socially conscious South Americans.

The market place,
Cuidad Rodrigo

In Madrid I once went to an exhibition of Inca jewellery lent by the Peruvian Government – an astonishing collection of beautiful things, necklaces and animal figures, great beaten breastplates or dream-like headgears. I watched the Spaniards closely as they wandered around these treasures, and found that they had inherited in full degree the instincts of the conquistadores: like those blood-and-thunder connoisseurs, they did not much bother about the aesthetics, but ran their fingers instantly down the catalogue, as they examined each object in turn, to find its precise weight in gold. And more subtly suggestive still of *Hispanidad*, of the paradoxical physical resemblance between Old Spain and New, is the sight of a sheep-herd on its way to market, along one of the dirt roads that wind through the mountains of western Castile. You can see the sheep from miles away, surrounded in their haze of dust, and hear the barking of the dogs and the whistles of the herdsmen; and as they advance across that bare dry landscape, their white mass now spreading, now coalescing, it is the easiest thing in the world to fancy that you are back with Pizarro in the Andean foothills, that Cuzco, not Segovia, lies over the hill, that there is a smell on the wind not of wild daffodils, but of coca, and that the animals approaching you are not sheep of Castile, but long-necked ruminative llamas, hastening with a pad of cameloid hoofs towards the City of the Sun.

One of the plaintive melodies sung by Spanish workmen may, if you hear it one morning from your bedroom window, strike you as vaguely familiar. It is a sad song about a nobleman's search for his dead wife, and the Spaniards took it with them to the Americas. During the great gold rush of 1849 the Mexican miners in California sang it so incessantly that their American and English colleagues learnt it too, parodied it, gave it a new set of words and called it 'My Darling Clementine'.

The most improbable Spaniards, dyed by this martial past, often have something soldierly about them. I once came across a bust, in a garden-plaza of Ciudad Rodrigo, which I at first assumed to represent the Duke of Wellington, who won a famous victory there – so proud and commanding was its eroded stone face, so bravely decorated its uniform with braid and laurel wreaths. I asked a passing woman, however, just to make sure, and found I had been mistaken: that was no general, she said, but a well-known organist of Salamanca Cathedral – a saintly man, and a musician of universally respected talent. I ought not to have been surprised. In every Spanish music-case there lies a pair of batons.

In Spain nobody can quite escape the bugle-calls, and the emblems of war are everywhere. It may be an antique figure on a Salamanca tomb, the man in all the panoply of mediaeval arms, the woman dressed in the nun's costume which she swore to wear throughout his absence at the battles. It may be a place of arms: the little mosque, beside the fairground at Granada, in which Ferdinand negotiated the surrender of Boabdil, the last Moorish king in Spain; or the bridge down the road from where the Catholic Monarchs watched their flag rise at last above the towers of the Alhambra. It may be the pockmarks of old gunfire, like the holes of the French shells all over the Torre del Cuarto in Valencia, or the scarred nave of the Romanesque cathedral of Lérida, which used to be a machine-gun range. It may only be some quirk of combat, like the gilded screen in Toledo Cathedral which was coated with iron to hide its value from Napoleon's looters, and has never been scraped clean. It may be the sarcophagus

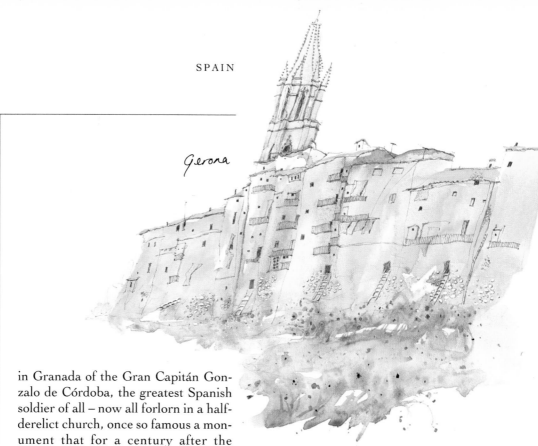

Gerona

in Granada of the Gran Capitán Gon-
zalo de Córdoba, the greatest Spanish
soldier of all – now all forlorn in a half-
derelict church, once so famous a monument that for a century after the
general's death a hundred banners flew daily over his tomb.

But more terribly, it may be a reminder of that last and worst of the
Spanish wars, which tore this country apart in the thirties, and left it
half hushed and numbed until only the other day: a broken bridge,
perhaps; a row of crosses; the little cork grove, near Salamanca, where
General Franco became the Caudillo; or some shabby city of the north,
Gerona, Vich, or Tortosa, over whose cobble-streets and dowdy
houses even now there seems to hang some residual ignominy of
defeat.

8
CHRIST
THE KING

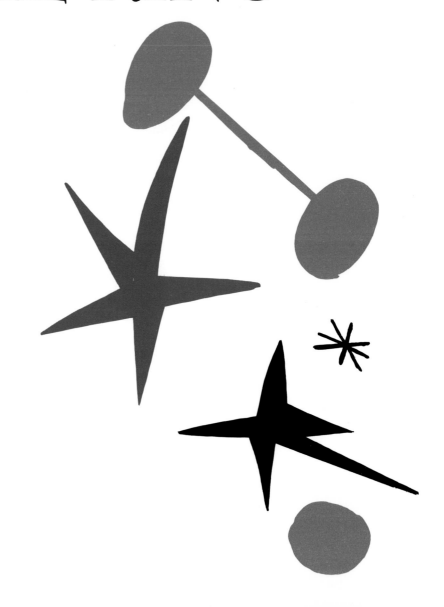

The Gothic cathedral at León is one of the few in Spain that feel *light* – the Spaniards did not share the French taste for glass walls, and preferred a brawnier, grimmer style. León has a vast amount of marvellous glass, no *coro* to obstruct the central view, and a general sense of lucidity; and as if to exploit this feeling of revelation, the chapter has enclosed the west end of the nave with an enormous sheet of plate glass, enabling the tourist to press his nose against the window when a service is actually taking place inside.

This is an astonishing sensation. Immediately in front of you, a foot or two beyond the glass, an elderly Spanish canon will be sitting before his missal in all the glory of his golden vestments – champing at the mouth a little, perhaps, or fidgeting with his stole, so close that you can almost smell the cough-drops on his breath or turn over the pages for him. To right and left, embedded in their stalls, the other canons sit reverently engrossed, birettas hung on the walls behind; and at the lecterns below them, rising and sitting in antiphony, two young precentors chant the liturgy – churchmen of immense enthusiasm, like up-and-coming barristers, who throw their whole physiques into their devotions, and do not neglect, now and then, to cast a swift glance behind them, to see how that profane audience behind the glass is behaving itself. It is almost like being a Spanish priest yourself, to stand so close to those vivacious canonicals; or perhaps you may be reminded, without

León Cathedral

irreverence, of the great aquaria in America, through whose thick portholes you may squint to see the poor dolphins sporting themselves inside.

Spain is a Christian country in the way that Saudi Arabia is Muslim, Burma Buddhist, or Russia Communist. To the average citizen of the West, with his pagan or humanist social background, her Christianity is as exotically mysterious as any faith of fetish or of ancestry. Church and State may no longer be virtually synonymous, as they were in Franco's day (the Caudillo was *ex officio* a canon of Astorga), but for centuries the Catholic Church has been one of the ruling forces of Spain, and even now, the moment you set foot within her frontiers the tokens of the creed are as ubiquitous as prayer-wheels in Nepal. Christianity was for generations the binding force of this centrifugal nation. It was in the name of Christ that the Catholic Monarchs united Spain, earning for this country, by Papal Bull, the perpetual right to eat meat on Fridays. In a sculptured relief in Granada Cathedral Ferdinand and Isabel are shown accepting the surrender of Granada with their spiritual adviser, Cardinal Mendoza, so powerful a prelate that he was known as Tertius Rex; and it is properly symbolic, perhaps, that of the three, only the Cardinal is wearing gloves. It was in the cause of Christian unity that the Jews and the Moors were expelled – the Jews because of their 'continual attempts to divert and turn faithful Christians from our holy Catholic faith, taking them away from it and drawing towards their own diseased beliefs and opinions'. The ships of the conquistadores crossed the Atlantic loaded deep with crosses, missionaries, missals, and Christian convictions, and Spain in her heyday saw herself as the champion of Christian orthodoxy, whose task it was

Granada Cathedral

to unite the world in Catholicism; it was the defeat of the Armada by the English Protestants, in 1588, that cracked her confidence in her mission and herself.

In the Spanish context Christianity has always meant power and purpose. Within this stronghold, a heretic is traditionally a fifth columnist – and indeed, five centuries after the fall of Granada it was a Spanish Christian general who coined that very phrase, to describe the secret body of sympathizers who would help the four Nationalist columns to seize Madrid for the faith. For the faith! As the whole course of the Reconquest was partly a war and partly an act of devotion, so to many Nationalists the Civil War, which brought Franco's regime to power, was the last of the holy wars. The Republic had rashly tried to break the Church's hold on education, and generally to separate religion from Government; the war memorials of their opponents usually describe the dead as having laid down their lives 'for God and for Spain'. 'Commend your soul to God,' cried Moscardó to his son, over the telephone line from the Alcazar, 'shout *Viva España*, and die like a hero' – and thus he summed up the three estates of Christian *casticismo*, universal, patriotic, individual. The decisive moments of Spanish history have always occurred when Christianity has, by force or persuasion, welded the nation into one of its periods of purpose. One such moment was that *annus mirabile*, 1492, when the last Moors were defeated, the Jews were expelled, and the Cross first set sail, beside the Spanish flag, for the Americas. Another such moment, you may like to remind yourself as you peer through the plate glass at León, has only just come to an end.

This does not mean that every Spaniard goes to Mass. Before the Civil War it was estimated that only a third of the population confessed or communicated; today the proportion is probably less than half, with women predominating. Anti-clerical feeling in Spain, as distinct from anti-religious feeling, has often been violent. Church and power have so often gone together – 'Money is very Catholic', says a bitter Spanish proverb – and though the association of the two has done some great things for Spain, it has also helped to sour the attitude of the poor

towards organized religion. The saddest statues in Europe are the mutilated figures of saints outside Tortosa Cathedral, which look as though they were hacked about by Cromwellian troopers or Muslim fanatics, but were in fact desecrated by furious citizens of modern Spain, half a century ago.

The Spanish Church has always been proud, and frequently independent. Its bishops have seldom been flaccidly subservient towards the Vatican, and in our own time the gentle Pope John XXIII so disapproved of Spanish policies that when a distinguished ex-Minister was nominated to represent this Christian State at the Holy See, his accreditation was refused (and he killed himself). Spain is a much more sceptical, ironic country than Italy, say, and within her frontiers the faith seems to have wider limits than elsewhere. At one end we have the severe intellectuals of the hierarchy, whose pale ascetic faces you may see in any Spanish cathedral, absorbed in their books in the dim-lit *coro*, or scattering like a meteor shower after vespers – each to his own small chapel in the transept, and thence through a little door into the evening light. I once walked into the cathedral of La Seo in Saragossa to find in progress the public examination of a newly nominated canon, and never did I feel more strongly the intellectual iron of Catholicism. In the background there hovered a couple of choirboys in surplices, and a stoop-shouldered beadle in a mouldy wig. At a table behind the *coro* the young canon was reading his thesis with gusto, speaking very fast about one of the abstruser theological conceptions, and sometimes emphasizing his point with a gentle slap of his hand upon the table. And bundled mysteriously on their benches before him were his seniors of the

Interior, cathedral of La Seo, Saragossa

152

chapter, screwed up in cassocks, embroidered surplices, and stoles, one facing this way, another that, and all looking immensely old, eminent, and saintly. At first I thought these wrinkled objects were fast asleep; but I tiptoed across the aisle to their benches, and as I approached them I noticed that first one watery old eye, then another, then a third, was fastened upon me with an expression of infinitely lively awareness. I withdrew abashed, and there pursued me towards the door the tap of the beadle's censorious wand, and the rich voice of the candidate, pressing home a dogma.

At the other end stand all those miraculous relics which, to the cold northern mind, blur the edge between religion and superstition, and give to Spanish Catholicism an odour of wizardry. All over Spain there are miracle-working images of the Virgin, hallowed and well-loved objects with traditional powers of cure and protection. They are usually squat, primitive, vaguely Oriental figures, blackened by centuries of candle smoke, and sitting upon their high plinths, their banks of flowers, or their altars like dark little idols. Most of them are mediaeval figures which were buried for their safety when the Moors conquered Spain, whose whereabouts was forgotten during the seven centuries of Muslim rule, and whose rediscovery after the Reconquest was regarded as miraculous. A typical story is that of the Black Virgin of Montserrat. This small, almost African-looking image, now to be seen as a small black blob among the multitudinous flowers, gems, and candles of its altar, was discovered by some shepherds who noticed strange lights flickering, to celestial music, outside a cave on the holy mountains; a sweet fragrance surrounded the image, a halo hovered about its head, and when they carried it down the steep mountain track it presently grew so strangely heavy that they left it where it was, and built around it a monastery that is famous now wherever Christianity is known.

Others claim a genesis even more remarkable. The Virgin of the Forsaken, the patroness of Valencia, was carved in the fourteenth century as the emblem of a charitable society; legend says that it was made by a group of pilgrims who asked the society for four days' supply of food and a sealed room, and who disappeared without a trace, leaving the image behind them and thus proving themselves to have been, beyond all reasonable doubt, angels. Our Lady of Guadalupe, whose monastery stands in a slouching mediaeval village in Estremadura, was discovered by a herdsman in the thirteenth century. A dead cow he was skinning suddenly came to life again, and as it staggered to its feet, so there appeared beside it a vision of the Virgin, who said that if they dug on the spot where the cow had lain, there they would find a miraculous image: they did, and Our Lady of Guadalupe presently became so famous that half the Kings of Spain paid homage to her, Don John of Austria gave her Ali Pasha's stern lantern after the Battle of Lepanto, Columbus named an island for her, and she possesses a wardrobe of several thousand dresses, marvellously worked and studded with precious stones.

There is something very touching to these old legends, and something moving to the devotion that simple people still accord to these antique objects. Occasionally, though, an element more eerie creeps into a cult. One of the more alarming examples, to my mind, is the Virgin of the Pillar at Saragossa, which owes its fame to an apocryphal journey to the city by the ubiquitous St. James. On January 2nd in the year 40, we are told, St. James was visited at Saragossa by a vision of Our Lady, who descended from Heaven upon a pillar of jasper. Around this pillar, and the fifteenth-century figure of the Virgin that now surmounts it, a formidable Basilica has been erected. It is a severe rectangular building, with four tall towers and a central tumble of cupolas, and its pinnacles rise like watchtowers above the Ebro, dominating the plain of Aragón. It stands there rather like a Spanish Kremlin, and its interior is dark, mysterious, and very stuffy, as if no fresh air has been admitted for centuries, and all is stale breath, incense, and candle smoke.

High upon her pillar the Virgin stands, set against a background of indescribable glitter – she is said to be adorned with 8,000 diamonds, 145 pearls, 74 emeralds, 62 rubies and 46 sapphires. Around her people are always praying, priests are always hurrying, incense is always swirling, and sightseers are always mutely staring. She has been there for at least five centuries, and in those years, we are assured, there has not been a single daylight moment when she has been alone. It is not, though, these activities of devotion that give her

Jaén Cathedral

shrine its chill fascination. It is something older and darker, something pre-Christian perhaps, that puts you in mind of magic and moonlight. Near the shrine there hang two unexploded bombs, which were dropped on this cathedral by the Republicans during the Civil War, but miraculously failed to explode – the Virgin had been officially appointed Captain-General of the city. And behind it, below that compartment into which the priests clamber to change her costumes or her jewellery, like dresses at an opera – through a small aperture behind you may see a small bare portion of the holy pillar itself. All day long the pilgrims pause at this spot, to stoop in the dark and kiss that piece of stone. The atmosphere is thick and queerly hushed around them, the candles flicker through the sickly lilies, somewhere a Mass is being said, and nobody has ever broken it to those devotees that St. James never came this way at all, nor ever saw Our Lady beside the Ebro.

Perhaps it is true now, because so many people have believed it so long – thousands of Spanish girls are christened Pilar in honour of the Saragossa Virgin. Certainly there is to the more atavistic symbols of Christianity in Spain a dignity that comes not from themselves, but from the centuries of devotion, respect, and fear they have inspired. One of the best-loved figures in Spain is that called the Christ of the Plain, which hangs in the little Basilica of St. Leocadia below the walls of Toledo. Before this image, we are told, a young peasant girl and her faithless betrothed once asked Our Lord to arbitrate between them; the sad, emaciated figure above the altar lowered its right arm from the Cross to acquit the girl – and thus the arm hangs still, in the seclusion of the little church, down on the plain beside the arms factory. Another pleasant legend is illustrated in the fine cathedral of Santo Domingo de la Calzada, in Old Castile. In this small city, long ago, a young man who had been wrongly hanged for theft miraculously came to life again upon the gallows, and the bystanders hastened off to the Mayor to have him cut down; the Mayor was having his dinner, and was just about to start work on the two plump roast chickens that lay on the table before him when the disconcerting news arrived. 'Nonsense!' he cried. 'You might just as well say that these two birds on my dinner table could get up and crow!' Need I end the tale? They crowed to such effect that to this very day, in a kind of gilded coop inside the cathedral, two live white chickens, a cock and a hen, perpetuate their memory; they do an eight-day shift, but are excused duty in the winter because the building gets too cold.

In the cathedral of Barcelona there is a figure of Our Lord which is oddly twisted in the trunk; this, we are told, was taken to Lepanto by Don John, and twisted itself in the course of the action to evade a Turkish cannon-ball. In León Cathedral stands the Madonna of the Die: an unlucky gambler once threw his dice at this figure, and was horrified to find that the nose of the Christ Child began to bleed in pro-test. In the agreeable little cathedral of Santander the heads of two local martyrs are kept in an illuminated socket in the front of the high altar; their skulls are fitted with silver replicas of their faces, and when

I once asked the sacristan when they were martyred, he assured me kindly that it was 'many years ago', as though I was afraid they might not be quite dead yet. In Valencia Cathedral there is a graceful goblet which is claimed to be the Holy Grail – and which indeed, though it was made some centuries after the Last Supper, really did inspire many of those deeds of devotion that created the Grail's legend, and thus is the true progenitor of Morte d'Arthur and Lohengrin. In the cathedral of Oviedo, preserved in a kind of deposit-crypt, a splendid eleventh-century coffer contains two thorns from Christ's crown, a sandal of St. Peter's, several pieces of the Cross, and one of the thirty pieces of silver – saved from the Moors by subterfuge, and from Napoleon's troops by bribery.

There are two handkerchiefs in Spain claiming to be St. Veronica's: one in the monastery of Santa Clara, outside Alicante, the other lying in an urn above the high altar of Jaén Cathedral, supported by golden cherubs and reached by pilgrims by means of a wooden ladder behind. An entire wall of a chapel in the monastery at Loyola, the birthplace of St. Ignatius, is covered with relics of the saint, from his bones to his gloves; as for St. Theresa, her poor body was exhumed some years after her death, and broken into miracle-working relics that are now scattered across Christendom. There are 7,500 holy relics inside the Escorial, including the sacred wafer which, so Augustus Hare darkly tells us, 'bled at Gorcum when trampled on by Zwinglian heretics'; high on one of the central towers, if you look carefully from the north side, you may see a small rectangle of gilded bronze, said by some to contain the veil of St. Barbara, and certainly covered with invocations against lightning.

The *ex votos* of Spain are often fascinating. Sometimes

The cathedral of Santo Domingo de la Calzada, Old Castile

157

they are only wax heads, limbs, or little figures, but often they are crudely painted pictures of escapes or recoveries – sick men rising from their beds, muleteers narrowly escaping trains at level crossings, appalling car accidents in which the grateful donor is miraculously thrown clear, X-ray pictures of needles in children's stomachs, water-colours of people being gored by bulls, caught in revolving water-wheels, falling in fires, thrown off horses down precipices, or rescued from certain drowning, sunk as they are in the troughs of gigantic seas, by visions of Our Lady above the storm clouds. Even animals are sometimes remembered: in Oviedo Cathedral there is a statue of St. Anthony with his pig, symbolic of the earthly possessions he has renounced, and always hung around his waist are five or six small wax piglets, placed there in gratitude by peasants who assume him to be the Patron of the Sty. All over Spain there are statues whose feet are worn smooth by kissing, or whose heads shine from the touch of countless reverent hands, through several centuries of Christian certainty. The toes of a figure of San Pablo de Alcántara, which was erected outside Cáceres Cathedral only in 1954, are already rubbed smooth and brassy by the faithful; as for that statue of Maestro Mateo in the portico of Santiago, so many people have bumped foreheads with it, in search of inspiration, that it has a perceptible dent between the eyes.

And the oddest of all these manifestations is not a miracle at all, not even a very holy image, but only a clever piece of theatrical mechanics. If you go to Mass one Friday morning in the Church of Corpus Christi in Valencia, you will notice above the altar a fine picture of the Last Supper by Francisco Ribalta. At the climax of the service, while the choir sings the Miserere, there is a slight whirring and creaking noise from the recess behind the altar, and this picture suddenly vanishes – to be replaced first by blue vel-vet curtains, which are drawn to reveal black velvet cur-tains, which are drawn to reveal in a moment of unde-niable excitement, a vividly

Oviedo Cathedral

illuminated life-size crucifix. The choir sings softly throughout this phenomenon, the congregation is on its knees, a genuine sense of drama emanates from the mechanism, and it is easy to see that not so very long ago, to the breathless peasants of the Valencia plain, it must have seemed proof positive that Christ was born to die for us.

Sleight of hand indeed, but in Spain the Church is dealing with a populace in whose minds, even now, the Christian faith is inextricably confused with older values. 'The Spaniards are good Christians,' a Venetian ambassador once observed, 'but immoral.' Where their pagan superstitions end, and where their Christianity begins, the most sophisticated candidate for canonry could scarcely begin to demonstrate.

Sometimes, though, beliefs and customs can be directly traced to the rites of paganism. At Mérida, the old Roman fortress-city, an elegant shrine to the god Mars has been turned into a chapel in honour of the child-martyr St. Eulalia – said to have been roasted on the spot in the reign of Diocletian. It is customary for the women of Mérida to toss locks of their hair through the chapel grille from the pavement outside, and the little building is regarded with such veneration that often you see people on the other side of the street, staid young couples or solitary old gentlemen, standing stock-still in prayer and contemplation before it. One evening I was standing before its grille, half lost in meditation myself, when I heard pants and footsteps beside me: two small girls in red coats were crossing themselves at my side, and when I looked down at them they hastily pressed their thin arms through the grille, dropped two pink-ribboned pigtails on the floor before the altar of Mars, crossed themselves again, and ran quickly home through the street lights.

Pagan or Christian? I do not know which to think the great fiestas of Spain, which have become, through the medium of tourist pamphlet and travel agency, as emblematic of this country as the *Folies Bergères* used to be of Paris. Marvellously varied is the form of these great displays. In some parts of Andalusia they lead lambs through the streets on strings, to celebrate Easter morning. In Catalonia, on Corpus

Christi Sunday, they create elaborate patterns of petals in the city streets. To celebrate the feast of St. Joseph in Valencia, they build vast effigies of characters fictional, real, or symbolical, and burn them in a final wild orgy at midnight. On the feast of St.Fermín, in Pamplona, they let young bulls loose in the streets, and allow the youths of the city, gay in the yellow sashes of Navarre, to pit their courage against their horns.

The greatest of the fiestas are the Passion Week processions of Andalusia. There are few spectacles on earth to match the holy parades of Málaga or Seville – events all the more haunting because their strangeness, dignity, and reverence are coupled with an odd matter-of-fact detachment, as though the whole affair is only one more job in the daily round, like catching the morning bus or doing the shopping. Imagine such an evening of display, in such a city of the Spanish South. It is almost certain to be warm – Málaga claims the finest climate in Europe, with the lowest rainfall. It is almost certain to be sticky, for so many people come south for Easter week that rents go up all along this southern littoral, and if you want a hotel room for a night you may have to book it for the whole week. It is almost certain to be slightly disorganized, for though the Spaniards are masters of crowd control, the only function they ever begin on time is the bull-fight – whose crowds will clap and catcall if the opening trumpet is a moment late.

The pavements, then, are packed and jostling, the ice creams and fizzy drinks are selling well, the big-wigs are looking grand but uncomfortable upon their chairs of honour, and presently there advances at a funereal pace along the avenue one of the strangest of all processions. An equestrian officer leads it, perhaps, sword drawn and medals dangling, but hard at his heels there pace the penitents, living survivals of the old flagellating sects, grouped by fraternity, with tall conical hoods upon their heads, narrow slits for their eyes, wands in their hands, and bright silken gowns – crimson, blue, or white – trailing about their ankles. They move in singular movements, looking warily from side to side, for their hoods obscure their vision; and with the swaying motion of the head that this gives them, together with a general manner of casual, swaggering, lordly menace, they look like eerie travesties of regimental drum-majors, parading down some very different Mall.

Lines of infant penitents follow them, jollied along by young priests, and chewing gum to keep them on their feet; a band may come next, playing the sombre hymns of Passion Week; and then there lurch into sight, grotesque and towering in the lamplight, the great floats that are the purpose of the procession – vast gilded images of Our Lord or the Virgin Mary, elaborate with palm trees or tabernacles, decked in flowers, candles, and carpets, carried by ranks of bent-backed, panting, cowled or cassocked men. A hooded major-domo keeps them in time, walking backwards before them and clanging a bell, and every few paces they have to stop, so enormous is the weight of the floats; and so in a sad and dreadful rhythm, to the muffled beat of a drum, they make their slow way through the city streets, so high, so ornate, so heavy, so queer, with the hoods of those penitents, the beat of that drum, the smell of the flowers on the air and the flicker of the candles, that the most tremendous of military parades, the tanks in Red Square or the Garde Républicaine down the Champs Élysées, pale in the imagination beside them.

Occasionally a woman standing in the crowd, or leaning from some high balcony, breaks into the hard thrilling notes of a *saeta* – an arrow-song of mourning or remorse which she projects like a missile towards the passing image. Such interventions are mostly prearranged, however, and if you are close enough to the procession you will see that when those floats stop for a rest the men who carry them, stretching their backs and flexing their muscles in relief, often wave cheerfully to a friend in the crowd, exchange a few words of badinage with some hooded apparition, call jokingly for a Coca-Cola, or even light up a cigarette. They smell of sweat. They sometimes grumble. They are, one feels, only on contract to tradition, and old gods of atavism have signed their work-sheets.

Outside the monastery
in Holy Week, Guadalupe

'Speak Cleanly! Law, Morality, and Decorum Alike Forbid Blasphemy.' So it says above the public washhouse on the waterfront at Corunna, and until a few years ago all it implied was true. Not only did Decorum and Morality prohibit Blasphemy, but the Law did too: not only was the Christian Church confessor and comforter to the people, it was also Authority. Today the old grip on public conduct has been broken. The ever-visible multitude of priests, monks and nuns, which used to give Franco's Spain an almost Tibetan feeling, is less apparent now. The Church itself stands uncertainly amidst the whirl of change: what would the bishops have thought in Franco's day, to see the young couples publicly embracing in the Plaza Mayor in Madrid, or find the lurid girlie magazines upon the bookstalls of Seville?

The death of Franco, the fall of his values, left Spain eager for all the liberties, including liberty of morals, so that within a year or two few countries in western Europe seemed more permissive. But it was deceptive in a way. The old standards were only out of fashion, and all over Spain, at any moment of any day, the old ways and rituals still

The Cathedral of La Sagrada Familia, Barcelona

proceeded. The X-certificate films might be packing the houses in Madrid, but at a thousand churches up and down the country a service was being conducted, if only for a congregation of two or three. In dozens of seminaries the pale young students still learnt their Latin. In scores of closed convents the nuns were praying. In many a village a local saint's day was being celebrated, and the first communicants were walking home from church in bridal gowns and sailor suits; more than 1,500 saints are honoured in the Spanish calendar, and each has his fervent

Doorway to the monastery of Las Batuecas

devotees. ('He's not a saint,' sniffed a caretaker when I asked the identity of a holy man buried in Santo Domingo de la Calzada, *'he's only a Blessed!'*) On the north tower of Astorga Cathedral, on the north-east tower of the Cathedral of the Pillar at Saragossa, on the dizzy pinnacles of Gaudi's Church of the Sagrada Familia at Barcelona, on the staid mock-Gothic of the cathedral of Madrid – on all these great Christian structures, and many more, the builders were hammering and the cranes clanking. At the bull-ring the priest stood by for human casualties outside the little whitewashed chapel, and in a remote and lovely corner of Las Hurdes, a wild landscape of west Castile long supposed to be inhabited only by demons, the shy Carmelites of the monastery of Las Batuecas, locked away behind their high walls, had written beside their door-bell: 'Brother! This is not a place of Tourism or Diversion! Unless you have Real Need, do not Ring this Bell!'

Did not God say, in the vision of the Great Promise, that Spain was a chosen land? Is she not still a nation of saints, mystics, hermits and evangelists? (St. Francis Xavier, the greatest missionary of them all, came – as the Spaniards would say – from a very good family in Navarre.) Was it not Spain, in our own lifetimes, that Paul Claudel apostrophized in his poem *Aux Martyres Espagnols* – 'sixty thousand priests massacred and not one apostasy'?

I dare say that Spain, now that she is launched on the libertarian path, will never be *quite* so Christian again. The decrees of the churchmen will never be so absolute, and the Church itself will never again be so formidable an estate of the realm. The loyalty of many centuries, though, does not wither in a generation, especially when it is shot through with faith: there may yet be a time when the Spaniards look once more to the Catholic Church, as they did in the days of the Reconquest, to lead them out of alien tyrannies, or give them pride again.

9
FOUR CITIES

It is especially in the interior of Spain that the faith still rings true, for though Christianity is more ebullient in the south, the stern landscapes of the tableland are like sounding-boards for the spirit. Here, though your voice often falls flat upon a dry soil, or is whisked away by the bitter wind, ideas seem to echo and expand, visions form in the great distances, and man, all alone in the emptiness, seems only the agent of some much greater Power. No wonder the Spaniards, at once oppressed and elevated by the character of the place, have built upon this plateau some of the grandest of all human artifacts, the cities of the centre. They are grand not so much as collections of treasures, or gatherings of people, but as things in their own right: all different, all indeed unique, all instantly recognizable for their own savour and design, but all touched by this same resonance of setting, and thus, one feels, by something nobler still. Let us visit four of them now, and see how powerfully this combination of variety and inner cohesion contributes to the presence of Spain.

Salamanca, on the western edge of the *meseta*, is made of sandstone. One does not often specify the raw material of a city, but Spain likes to be explicit: Santiago is granite, Salamanca is sandstone. She is the calmest of the famous cities of the tableland, set more tranquilly than most beside the River Tormes, insulated by age and culture against the

The Roman bridge and the cathedral, Salamanca

fierce intensity of the country. Salamanca is above all a university city – 'Mother of the Virtues, the Sciences, and the Arts' – and though her scholarship has long been shrivelled, her colleges decimated in war or emasculated by autocracy, still she has the special poise that marks a place both learned and long admired.

You approach her, if you come the right way, by foot across a fine Roman bridge, and this in itself is a kind of sedative. The bridge is old, stout, and weather-beaten; the river below is wide and steady; groves of larches and poplars line the banks; and if you pause for a moment at the alcove in the middle, you will find that life around you seems wonderfully simple and assured, as though the big trucks pounding along the ring road are only some transient phenomenon from another civilization. In the thicket immediately below the bridge, perhaps, a solitary student is deep in his book at a trestle table, supported by a bottle of pop from the shanty-café along the path, and inspired by flamenco music from the radio beneath his chair. Downstream the bourgeoisie washes its cars in the river water. Across the river a small boy canters around on a pony. A mill-wheel turns at the weir upstream; sheep graze the fields beyond; in the shallows an elderly beachcomber is prodding the mud with a stick.

Raise your eyes only a little, and there above you, scarcely a stone's throw away, stand the two cathedrals of Salamanca – so close is the Spanish country to the Spanish town, so free from peevish suburbs are these old cities of the interior. It is rather like entering Oxford, say, in the Middle Ages. The city is the heart and the brain of its surrounding countryside, so dominant that the olive trees themselves seem to incline their fruit towards its market, and the mules and asses pace instinctively in its direction. Yet the physical break is instant, and complete. One side of the river is the country, the other side is the city, and there is no straggle to blur the distinction.

Almost immediately, too, the meaning of Salamanca becomes apparent, and you seem to know by the very cut or stance of the place that this is a city of scholars. Here is the old courtyard of the university, where generations of students have written their names in flowery red ochre; and here are bookshops, those rarities of contemporary Spain, heavily disguised with magazine racks and picture postcards, but still recognizably university shops; and here is the great mediaeval lecture-room of Luis de León, still precisely as he knew it, still bare and cold and dedicated, with his canopied chair just as it was when, reappearing in it after four years in the cells of the Inquisition, he began his lecture with the words *Dicebamus hesterna die . . .'* – 'As we were saying yesterday . . .'

Salamanca University was founded in the thirteenth century, and for four hundred years was one of the power-houses of European thought. Columbus's schemes of exploration were submitted to the judgement of its professors. The Council of Trent was a product of its thinking. The concept of international law was virtually its invention. The first universities of the New World, in Mexico and Peru, were based upon its statutes. It was while serving as Professor of Greek at Salamanca that Miguel de Unamuno, driven out of his mind by the atrocities of the Spanish Civil War, rushed into the street one day shouting curses on his country, later to die of grief.

Around this institution, over the centuries, a noble group of buildings arose, and stands there still in golden splendour. The gorgeous plateresque façade of the Patio de las Escuelas, with its dizzy elaborations, its busts of Ferdinand and Isabel, and its lofty inscription – 'The King and Queen to the University and the University to the King and Queen' – is a reminder of the importance of this place to the State, the Crown and the Church throughout the grand epoch of Spanish history. The New Cathedral, pompous and commanding, was opened in 1560 to express the grandeur of a university that then boasted twenty-four constituent colleges, six thousand students, and sixty professors of unsurpassed eminence. One of the most delightful buildings in Spain is the House of the Shells, built at the end of the fifteenth century for a well-known Salamanca sage, and covered all over with chiselled scallops. And nothing in Europe better expresses a kind of academic festiveness than the celebrated Plaza Mayor, the drawing-room of Salamanca: its arcaded square is gracefully symmetrical, its colours are gay without being frivolous, its manner is distinguished without being highbrow, and among the medallions of famous Spaniards that decorate its façade there have been left, with a proper donnish foresight, plenty of spaces for heroes yet to come.

It is a lovely city, but like many lovely Spanish things, it is sad. Its glories are dormant. Its university, once the third in Europe, is now classed as the seventh in Spain, and seems to have no life in it. Few outrageous student rebels sprawl in the cafés of the Plaza Mayor, no dazzling philosophical theories are emerging from these libraries and lecture-rooms. Expect no fire from Salamanca. The Inquisition dampened her first, and in our own time Franco's narrow notions fatally circumscribed her. The genius of this tableland is not friendly to liberty of thought: and just as Spain herself is only now headily experimenting with the freedom of ideas, so it will be a long time, I fear, before Salamanca rejoins the roster of Europe's intellectual vanguard.

There is sadness too in Avila, though of a different kind. This is a soldier's city, cap-à-pie, and when you approach it from the west over the rolling plateau almost all you see is its famous wall: a mile and a half of castellated granite, with eighty-eight round towers and ten forbidding gates. It looks brand new, so perfect is its preservation, and seems less like an inanimate rampart than a bivouac of men-at-arms, their helmeted front surveying the *meseta*, their plated rear guarding some glowing treasure within. It looks like an encampment of Crusaders on the flank of an Eastern hill: a city in laager, four thousand feet up and very chilly, with the smoke rising up behind the walls where the field kitchens are at work.

But inside those watchful ranks, no treasure exists. Avila is like an aged nut, whose shell is hard and shiny still, but whose kernel has long since shrivelled. Her main gate is by the mottled cathedral, whose apse protrudes into the wall itself, and around whose courtyard a dozen comical lions – the only light relief in Avila – hold up an

The Gate of the Carmelites, Avila

iron chain, their rumps protruding bawdily over the columns that support them. At first the shell feels full enough, as you wander among the mesh of mediaeval streets inside, through the arcades of the central plaza, and down the hill past the barracks; but presently the streets seem to peter out, the passers-by are scarcer, there are no more shops, the churches tend to stand alone in piles of rubble, and the little city becomes a kind of wasteland, like a bomb-site within the walls, several centuries after the explosion.

Avila was always a mystic city, but this wasted presence gives her a gone-away feeling. The snow-capped sierra stares down at her, the plain around seems always to be looking in her direction, the little River Adaja runs hopefully past her walls; but when you knock at her gate, there is nobody home – and even those knights-at-arms turn out to be made of stone, and are floodlit on festival days. The life of the city has escaped the ramparts, and settled among the shops and cafés of the modern town outside; and from there, sitting with an omelette at a restaurant table, or wandering among the country buses, you may look up at the Gate of Alcazar and the city walls, and think how false, indeed how slightly ludicrous, a defensive posture can look when there is nothing at all to defend.

So emaciated does the old part of Avila feel today that sometimes it is difficult to imagine how virile she must have been in her palmy days. Was it really here that St. Theresa was born, that most robust of mystics, whose very visions were adventure stories, who jogged all over Spain in a mule wagon, and who did not even scruple to answer back Our Lord? ('That's how I treat My

The convent of St. Theresa, Avila

170

friends,' she once heard a divine voice remark, when she was complaining about a flooded river crossing, and unperturbed she retorted: 'Yes, and that's why You have so few!') Was it really in this pale outpost of tourism that young Prince Juan, only son of the Catholic Monarchs, was trained to rule the earth's greatest empire – only to die before his parents, and thus pass the crown to the house of Austria, to Philip II and his successors of the Escorial? Was it really in Avila, this city without a bookshop, that the great Bishop Alfonso de Madrigal, the Solomon of his time, wrote his three sheets of profound prose every day of his life – to be immortalized in the end by an alabaster figure in the cathedral that shows him halfway through his second page of the day? Was it here in Avila that the martyr St. Vincent, having stamped upon an altar of Jupiter, was beheaded on a rock with his two loyal sisters?

It all feels so remote, so long ago, so out of character: in the Civil War, the last great historical event in which Spain played a part, Avila fell bloodlessly to the Nationalists, and never thereafter heard a shot fired in anger. For me she is like a superb plaster cast of a city, all hollow. There is only one place in Avila in which the pungency of the past really seems to linger, and that is the crypt of the Church of San Vicente, just outside the walls on the eastern side. Here you may see the very rock on which that family of martyrs died, and beside it in the wall there is a small sinister hole. On October 27, 303, St. Vincent was executed, and his body was thrown to the dogs who prowled and yapped about the rock. A passing Jew paused to make fun of the corpse, but instantly there flew out of that small hole in the rock face an angry serpent, which threw itself upon the Hebrew and frightened him away. This episode was gratefully remembered by the Christians. For several centuries it was the custom of the people of Avila, when they wished to take an oath, to crowd down the steps of the crypt of San Vicente, and place their hands in that orifice as they swore; and to this day it is easy to see them down there in the dark, beside that rough old rock – awestruck peasant faces, queer hats and thonged sandals, a smell of must, earth, and garlic, a friar to supervise the solemnities and the slow words of the oath echoing among the shadows.

The Jew was so glad to escape with his life that it was he who built the church upstairs, and an inscription beside his tomb in the west transept tells the tale. As for the serpent, when Bishop Vilches took a false oath at the hole in 1456, out it popped again and stung him.

A world away is Segovia, and yet she stands only forty miles to the north-east, in the lee of the same mountains. If Avila is only a shell, Segovia is all kernel: she feels the most complete and close-knit of the Castilian cities, as though all her organs are well nourished, and nothing is atrophied. The gastronomic speciality of Avila is a little sweet cake made by nuns; but the speciality of Segovia is roast suckling pig, swimming in fat and fit for conquerors.

Segovia is the most beautifully organized of cities. She is a planner's dream. She lies along an elongated rocky knoll, with the sparse little River Clamores on the south side, and the more affluent Eresma to the north, and to get the hang of her you should first walk up to the little Calvary which stands, lonely and suggestive, on a hillock beside the Avila road. From there you can see the whole city in silhouette, and grasp its equilibrium. Very early in the morning is the best time, for then, when the sun rises over the plateau, and the city is suddenly illuminated in red, it loses two of its three dimensions, and looks like a marvellous cut-out across the valley. In the centre stands the tall tower of the cathedral, the last of the Gothic fanes of Spain. To the left there rise the romantic pinnacles of the Alcazar, most of it a nineteenth-century structure in the Rhineland manner, all turrets, conical towers, and trouba-

The Alcazar, Segovia

The Roman aquaduct, Segovia

dour windows, properly poised above a precipice (down which a four-teenth-century nanny, when she inadvertently dropped the baby, instantly threw herself too). And at the other end, forming a tremen-dous muscular foil to this fantasy, there strides across a declivity the great Roman aqueduct of Segovia, looking from this distance so powerful and ageless that it might actually be a strut to hold the hill up. Between these three bold cornerposts – fortress, church, and aqueduct – Segovia has filled herself in with a tight, steep, higgledy-piggledy network of streets, sprinkled with lesser towers, relieved by many squares, and bounded by a city wall which is often blended with houses too, and looks, from your brightening Calvary, rather like the flank of a great ship. She seems, indeed, to sail across her landscape. She looks like a fine old clipper ship, there in the morning sun, full-rigged, full-blown, ship-shape and Bristol-fashion.

A sense of strength or defiance infuses her. It was in the Alcazar that Isabel, recently proclaimed Queen of Castile, found herself besieged by a furious mob, but rode so bravely into the thick of it, alone upon her charger, that the crowd fell back subdued by her very presence. It was in the Alcazar too that the daring King Alfonso the Wise actually ventured to doubt, poring over his books one day, whether in fact the sun moved round the earth: instantly, such was the effect of this proposition, there was a flash of lightning, and the King, hastily dismissing the whole idea from his mind, ever afterwards wore a rope of St. Francis around his waist, a perpetual penance for a rash thought. It was in the queer little Church of Vera Cruz, beneath the castle, that the Knights Templar performed their secret rites of chivalry, standing vigil over their arms all night, in all the mysterious splendour of seneschal, gonfalon, and accolade. It was the image of our Lady of Fuencisla, in the Carmelite convent, that was officially made a Nationalist Field-Marshal in the Civil War; she still carries a Marshal's baton, and it is said that when Hitler was told the story, he swore that nothing on earth would induce him to visit Spain. Even the calamities of Segovia have a boisterous air: the old palace of the Alcazar, which was burnt down in 1862, was destroyed, it is said, by the cadets of its artillery school, because they wanted the school to be moved to Madrid. Even her miracles are thoroughgoing: one night in November 1602 an intense light shone over the convent of Santa Cruz, and the crowd that hastened there was gratified to find an eminent Dominican theologian, Melchor Cano, lost in prayer upon his knees, but suspended a good four feet above the level of the ground.

The finest sight in Castile, is how Segovians sweepingly define the first appearance of their city, and I agree with them: there can be few urban compositions on earth to equal the impact of Segovia, when you cross the last ridge on the approaching road, and see her bulk riding there above the fields. For myself, though, I remember with no less pleasure a stroll I took inside the city on my first evening there. It was a wet night, the lamplight shining damply on the streets, and as I wandered aimlessly through the drizzle I came upon a small plaza down the hill from the cathedral, called in the vernacular the Place of the Sirens. It is set upon a flight of steps, rather like the Scala d'Espagna in Rome, and feels like some slightly overpainted opera set – so theatrical that you almost expect it to revolve beneath your feet, to carry you onstage. To its left stands the lovely Romanesque atrium of San Martín, with a tall square tower above it; in its centre there stands the effigy of a well-known Segovian patriot, waving a flag; on the right, as you climb the steps, there is a row of enchanting small houses, ferns and flowers dripping over their balconies; above the rooftops there looms a foursquare fortified palace, where Wellingon stayed when he took Segovia; and at the top of the steps there is a small courtyard, enclosed on three sides by walls.

It was very shadowy in this yard that night, and I could not see very well. The street lights behind me, reflected in the puddles, only made the darkness darker. On the left-hand side, however, close to the wall, I could just make out two squat, plump stone shapes, crouching in the dark; and when I cautiously stumbled over to them, I found them to be a pair of queer primitive animals, with snouts, tails, and very solid bellies. Were they pigs? Were they lions? Were they gods? Were they devils? Nobody really knows, but I took no risks that evening, and hastily backed away from them: I was in Segovia, a city of spirit, and I thought they might bite.

Lastly Toledo, which stands to Spain as Kyoto to Japan – a repository of all that is proudest, oldest, and most private in the national consciousness. When you think of Old Spain, you think of Toledo – 'a clear and illustrious nightmare', as the poet Garcilaso de la Vega once irreverently described her. Toledo was once the capital of Spain, and is still the seat of the Spanish Primate, and within her walls the Castilian, Jewish, and Moorish cultures, productively co-existing for several centuries, created a rich and tolerant civilization of their own. Everybody knows what Toledo looks like, from El Greco's famous idealization of the place, and even the most determinedly flippant tourist, taking an afternoon excursion

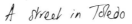

A street in Toledo

Toledo Cathedral

from Madrid, usually feels it necessary to cast an eye over this celebrated city, provided of course she can get back by cocktail time.

If you believed the old travellers you would imagine Spain to be one uninterrupted desert, absolutely denuded of vegetation; but Toledo is one city that really does live up to their descriptions – 'girdled in', as Augustus Hare put it, 'by the indescribable solitude of its utterly desolate hills'. She stands only forty miles from Madrid, but there *is* a kind of indescribable solitude to her flavour, and the desolation of her hills, if scarcely utter, still is severe. If Segovia often feels like a flat backcloth, Toledo is heavily in the round. She is built on a rocky mound in a bend of the Tagus, and is thus surrounded on three sides by a deep gorge, with shingle and grey rock running down to the water's edge. The river runs fast here, with a clutter of old stone mills and two excellent bridges; a castle stands sentinel across the stream; harsh grey hills are all about: the setting of Toledo is all abrasion – nothing soft, nothing amusing, nothing hospitable. This is the Spanish character at its most intractable. If a city can be said to look like a person, then Toledo looks just like one of those El Greco characters who were in fact conceived here – towering, handsome, humourless, sad, a little bloodless.

The Church dominates this city, and reminds us that the Archbishops of Toledo have often been men more powerful than the State itself: the formidable Cardinal Jiménez de Cisneros not only paid all the expenses of an expeditionary force to Africa, but actually led it himself, in the crimson. On the flank of Toledo's hill stands the fortress of the Alcazar, still recognizably large enough to hold, as it used to, two thousand horses in its subterranean stables. Unmistakably dominating it, though, its tower rising effortlessly above a tawny muddle of roofs and minor pinnacles, stands the cathedral. At night it is floodlit, and then the great luminous finger of this church, peremptory against the sky, makes even the transient sceptic think for a moment about immortality.

Inside the city, too, things of the spirit seem pre-eminent. They may be Jewish devotions that are remembered, in the haunted synagogues of this once-great Jewish city. They may be Muslim, in the adorable little mosque now called Cristo de la Luz – a tiny Córdoba, with its own small copse of horseshoe arches and its silent dusty garden. They may be memories of the Mozarabs, those Christians who retained their faith throughout the Moorish occupation, and thus kept alive the ancient liturgy of Gothic Christianity. When Toledo was recaptured from the Moors in 1085, a dispute arose as to whether the old Mozarabic rites should be retained, or replaced by the Gregorian rites from Rome – adopted in northern Spain during the years of the occupation. The issue was put to trial by fire. The rival prayer books were placed simultaneously in the flames, but the Roman was whisked to safety by a heavenly wind, while the Mozarabic simply did not burn; and because of this stalemate, which both sides claimed as a victory, the old Gothic ritual is still celebrated, every day of the week, in one chapel of Toledo Cathedral. (They keep the doors closed during the service, and when I chanced to open it one day I found myself almost at the priest's side on the steps of the altar: so severely did he turn to stare at me, so disapprovingly did his acolytes look up, so long and empty did the chapel extend behind him, that I instantly closed that door again, and allowed the Mozarabic ritual to continue its survival without me.)

But Roman or Gothic, Gregorian or Mozarab, above all it is Spanish Catholicism, that imperial creed, that is honoured and reflected in this imperial city. This is the city of the Toledo blade – 'a sword of Spain', as Shakespeare called it, 'the ice-brook's temper'; nowadays the swordsmiths make matadors' swords and paper knives, but once they were kept busy making swords for Christian knights. In the Church of Santo Tomé there hangs El Greco's celebrated picture *The Burial of Count Orgaz*, which epitomizes the alliance between God and the Spanish ruling classes. Count Orgaz was a Toledan so distinguished for piety that when he died the young St. Stephen and the old St. Augustine personally descended from Heaven to bury him. The painting shows them doing so, but more striking than their saintly figures are the Spanish gentlemen who stand behind. They look sorry indeed, but not surprised: they seem to represent a class of society that expect miracles as a matter of policy, and they are watching the saints at work rather as they might watch, with a certain patronizing interest, the technique of any foreign expert sent to do a job under reciprocal arrangements. To the right of the picture a priest appears to be checking the operation in some instruction handbook. High above, Philip II, though still alive when the painting was done, is already among his peers in Heaven. It is a beautiful picture, most richly composed, most haunting in portraiture, given an unexpected twinkle by El Greco's signature – Domenico Theotokopouli – delicately embroidered on the hem of a page's handkerchief; but it seems to record, not an instance of divine grace but the payment of a national due.

You may sense the same air of high collusion all over Toledo. At one end the Church of San Juan de Los Reyes, above the bridge of San Martín, is a resplendent monument to the Reconquest. Its architecture, the most delicate and elaborate kind of Gothic, is like a smile of gentle triumph across the prostrate art of the infidel, and upon its golden walls there hang the chains of Christian captives released from Moorish camps and galleys. At the other end of the city the ruined

Alcazar is a memorial, in many Spanish minds, to the last of the Crusades. 'The heroic epic,' said a message from the young women of Burgos to the defenders of the fortress in 1937, 'which your valour for God and Spain has written in our glorious Alcazar will be the pride of Spanish chivalry for ever': seventy priests had been murdered in Toledo, and when the Army of Africa fought its way in at last, the main street ran with blood, several wounded men were killed in their beds in hospital, and forty anarchists, trapped in a seminary, set fire to the building and burnt themselves to death.

And surveying all, the culmination of this city, Toledo Cathedral stands like a vast testimonial of Spain's devine destiny. The streets of Toledo are unbelievably tortuous, so narrow that along most of them a car cannot pass, and even a hand-trolley of oranges blocks the way; but when you have manoeuvred your baffled way along them, have discovered the unremarkable outer walls of the cathedral, and have entered its unobtrusive cloister gate, then the immense expanse of the interior, its nave of seven bays and its twenty-eight chapels, seems to express the ultimate escape of the Spaniard from himself, *via* glory, to infinity. 'Valour for God and Spain' fills this great church like incense; and as witness to the working relationship between the two you may be shown a small white stone, preserved behind a grille, upon which Our Lady actually set foot during a royal visit in 666.

Soldiers, saints, heroes, and great churchmen seem to populate Toledo Cathedral, and when there is a service at the high altar, with all the swift formality of its ritual, the bowing priests, the genuflecting servers, the bewigged attentive vergers, the clink of the censers, the gorgeous shimmer of copes and jewelled monstrances, the exchange of plainchant between altar, *coro*, and thundering organ – when the heart of the cathedral is filled with the sights and sounds of that tremendous spectacle, this really does feel like the nerve-centre of some formidable war machine, a bunker or a Pentagon, disposing its unseen forces in distant strategies. From the transept ceilings the Cardinals' hats hang rotting like battle-flags. In the Chapter House the faces of all the archbishops look back at you from their portraits like generals in a war museum. In the treasury the silver spheres, rings, breastplates, censers, and crucifixes glitter beneath their bright lights like State jewels.

Toledo

Above the high altar there stands the figure of a mysterious shepherd who, sent by God to help Spain, guided the Christians to victory over the Moors through the mists of Las Navas de Tolosa in 1212; only King Alfonso VIII saw the face of this man, and the King it was, we are told, who carved the figure.

It is a great hall of triumph, a victory paean for the Christian culture. A superb assembly of treasures here upholds the Christian ethos – grilles by the great Spanish masters of wrought iron; sculpture and stained glass by virtuosos from Holland, Italy, and France; paintings by Rubens, Velázquez, Van Dyck, Goya, El Greco, Bassano,

Giovanni Bellini; multitudes of stone angels, tombs of kings and pre-
lates, sudden shafts of sunlight through stained glass, a vast, tumbled,
restless, infinitely varied museum of the faith. Nothing in Christendom, I suspect, better expresses the militancy of the Church than the
retablo or reredos of Toledo, which rises in serried magnificence from
the high altar to the roof. It is fretted everywhere with stone canopies
and niches, and in a series of elaborate stone tableaux, like the set of an
experimental theatre, tells the New Testament story; with an endless
profusion of detail, and an inexhaustible imagination – with saints on
guard at each flank, and angels fluttering everywhere – with a gleam-
ing gold, and blue, and a glow of old stone – with an almost physical
movement upwards, up through the sweet mystery of the Nativity and
the splendour of the Ascension, up through a glittering field of stars in
a deep blue sky – up to the very rafters of the cathedral, where your
dazed eye reaches at last the supreme symbol of Calvary, portrayed
there in immense tragic grandeur at the very apex of Christian Spain.

With such a cause, one feels, with such a champion, no Christian
soldier could lose. We are, however, in Spain, where the last victory is
death itself – '*Viva la Muerte!*' was the battle-cry of the Falange in the
Civil War. A few feet away from that glorious reredos there stands the
tomb of the Cardinal-Archbishop Portocarrero, Viceroy of Sicily, Cardinal Protector of the Spanish Nation, Regent and Primate of Spain.
He died in 1719, and has been described as 'incapable, obstinate, and
perfectly selfish'; but on his tomb, by his own orders, there was inscribed the dry Spanish epitaph *Hic Jacet Pulvis, Cinis, et Nihil* – 'Here
Lies Dust, Ashes, Nothing'.

Incomparable old cities of the interior! No other towns on earth are
anything like them. They have no peers, no rivals, no imitators. A
circle a hundred miles across would contain them all; but you can
stand ten thousand miles from their walls, close your eyes and think of
Spain, and see them clear as sunlight still.

10
BARBER'S BASIN

Down the road – down any Spanish road – lies Madrid, which was no more than a village until Philip II made her his capital in 1561, and is still compact enough for the country to show at the end of many city streets. Her two most enviable possessions are an art gallery, the Prado, and a park, the Retiro, and she is the capital of Spain chiefly because she happens to stand in the middle. Madrid was founded, they say, as a Moorish fortress, in the days when Castile was a no-man's-land between the Christian north and the Islamic south, and her original function was only military. No roads crossed at her site, no great river flowed there, there were no shrines, mines, or historical memories. Philip, plucking her from this obscurity, made her a kind of Brasília for Spain – an earnest of the future and a symbol of unity. The disparate provinces were all to pay allegiance to her, centralizing the energies of the nation, and from her brave new offices of Government, equidistant from the Primate at Toledo and the King at the Escorial, the purity of Spain was to be maintained. Besides, it looks neat and logical to have your capital in the centre, and nothing pleases the Spaniard more than symbolical precision.

The height of human happiness, infatuated Madrileños like to say, must be to go to that part of Heaven from which there is a view of Madrid. Others may feel they can survive Paradise without her. Standing as she does high in the tableland, with the desert plateau at the end of her suburbs, and a climate of horrid extremes, Madrid can hardly help sharing the melancholy of Castile; and in the winter especially she seems a capital half frozen in the attitudes of a past generation. In the 1930s she had a universal symbolism. In her, as so often in Spain before, the passions of the world were demonstrated, and men everywhere could see themselves and their societies reflected in her agonies. It was this guinea-pig status that brought the young idealists 'to this plateau beneath the sky's grave manifold of stars', and placed Madrid at the very heart of the world's preoccupations.

Today she offers us no pattern of hope or warning. Her example fires nobody. To the world outside the future of Madrid makes very little difference. She is no longer one of the archetypal capitals, and contributes little to the great issues that inflame us now – issues of

Puerta de Alcalá,
Madrid

morality, diplomacy, or strategy that scarcely intrude upon this peripheral metropolis. Her tastes are those of Paris, London or New York the year before last. Yesterday's pop music blares through her streets. Her art is mostly derivative, and the only really original programmes on her television screens are bull-fights. There is hardly a single striking modern building in Madrid.

And yet Madrid is one of the raciest, noisiest, and most boisterous of all the capitals of Europe; and this is because economics has overtaken politics in Spain, and introduced change by the service door.

Upon Madrid herself change has fallen like a pile of concrete, for sky-scrapers now dominate the centre of the capital, and immense new housing estates, mile after mile, district after district, are extending the city limits ever further into the *meseta*. The last of the slums has almost vanished, and Madrid feels rich. Here are the headquarters of the powerful Spanish banks, whose huge central offices have almost banished from the pavements of the Calle de Alcalá the café life that once distinguished it – in the days when the bull-fighters had their own coffee-house, the liberal intellectuals theirs, the poets another, the generals a fourth. Here are the diplomatic offices of the Americans, whose vast payments in return for strategic favours have helped to revise the fortunes of Spain, and here too are the headquarters of the Directorate-General of Tourism, whose staggeringly successful efforts to bring foreign visitors to Spain have acted as a yeast, to ferment the outlooks of the Spaniards. From Madrid, herself a babel of ill-digested modernism, all rushing traffic and gaudy cinemas, you may see how the influences of material advance, channelled through the offices of Philip's capital, are whittling away at the insularity of the State.

Industry has done most to change Spain, and bring her in step with the world. This is because it was the lack of industry that kept her an anachronism for so long. Until the 1960s this was a country whose mores, by and large, had been neither invigorated nor corrupted by the industrial way, whose dignities were

A street in Madrid close to the Plaza Mayor

essentially pastoral and whose manners were those of men in direct and personal contact with the earth. The fundamentals of human life – food, shelter, procreation, God – had not been filtered through the industrial mesh of machinery and mass employment, and this helped to give the Spaniard his sense of individual importance. He was no cog, even in the serf-like employment of the great southern estates, even beneath the rigid authoritarianism of Franco's system. He was that most important thing, a man – an *hidalgo*, which means in the dictionary definition 'a generous or noble man', but is literally 'a son of something', a somebody.

It was this security of status that gave the Spaniard his dignity – but also kept him poor: now he is offered a chance to change it. Every year more Spaniards move to the cities, to work in the factories that are fitfully appearing all over Spain. Every year new technical schools turn more peasants into mechanics, more investment creates new industries, the rising standard of living creates more demand for manufactured goods. Every year the growing economic power of Europe, spilling over the Pyrenees, makes it more inevitable that this stubborn survivor of an earlier age must lower its barricades. Spanish industry is still patchy, often old-fashioned, and sometimes uneconomic; but the Spaniards have, for better or for worse, now plumped for materialism, and you may already see the dams, the new roads and railways, the steel mills and the power plants that are the props of the philosophy.

Diplomatically, too, Spain is reconciling herself to the norm. At the end of the Second World War Spain stood forlornly alone in Europe – her Fascist friends obliterated, her Communist enemies riding high, her democratic neighbours hostile and contemptuous. It was not the first time in history that she had endured such isolation, but nowadays self-sufficiency is no longer a stimulant for nations, and long before Franco's death Spain had begun the long, difficult haul towards acceptance by the world. Even then, before democracy released the aspirations of the great public, many Spaniards were declining to accept the innate superiority of *casticismo*. If we take money from the foreigners, the reasoning went, why not ideas too? If a dollar is good for a refinery, why not for a juke box? If liberal democracy did this for them, why not for us?

Now that the barriers are down, Spain moves almost headlong towards membership with the rest of us: but it is an ironic truth that the most spectacular of all the pressures for change in this deeply conservative society has not been economic ambition, or religious disillusion, or even political frustration, but the often unprepossessing example of the tourist trade. It was in the tourists that the Spaniards first recognized their future selves: in the hippies of the fifties and the blue-rinsed Senior Citizens, in the portly parade of the sunburnt Germans, in the girl secretaries hitch-hiking down from Stockholm, in the urbane French plumbers with luxurious trailers, in the lovers kissing on open beaches and the women in trousers screaming obscenities at their disrespectful young.

So this was the world, the Spaniards reasoned. Perhaps it could be more fun, after all, than *casticismo* let it seem.

So the Spaniards reached, early in the 1970s perhaps, that moment of catharsis that economists call a 'take-off' – the moment in a nation's history when its economy gets into the rhythm of expansion, and its people realize that life may actually be expected to improve. The death of Franco, and the almost immediate dismantlement of the whole apparatus of his despotism, symbolically sealed the event, and opened the way to successions of many sorts.

Already the manners of the Spaniards have drastically altered. The duenna is a vanished figure, you no longer see the lovers kissing awkwardly but romantically through the grilles of Andalusian windows, young people are freer, loyalties wider. Spanish women have always been more powerful in the land than you would think from their cramped circumstances – there was a woman professor at Salamanca in 1606, and the most remarkable Communist of the Civil War was the fiery Basque known as The Passion Flower. In the last few years, though, they have swept almost at a stride through all the stages of emancipation, violently shifting the social, political, intellectual and not least the moral balance of the nation – perhaps the most revolutionary of all the revolutionary changes that have hit this country in our time.

The Spaniards drink more beer than they used to, and less wine. They go rather less to the bull-fight, and far more to the *futbol*. The

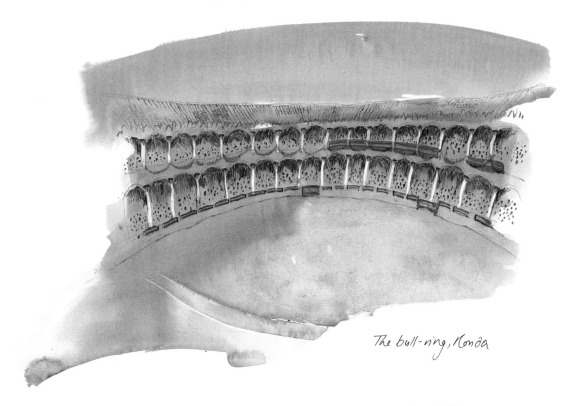

The bull-ring, Ronda

famous old bull-ring at Ronda, where the rules of the modern bull-fight were invented, is used as a cinema on off-season Saturdays. The traditional Spanish device called a *mesa de camilla*, a round table with a charcoal burner beneath it, can now be bought with electric heating. Old people still tend to disbelieve the possibility of your speaking a few words of Spanish, but children instantly understand you. The rock forms of the West often appeal to young Spaniards more than flamenco, and even at the Seville Feria you may find, in one or two of the festive pavilions, that the couples have abandoned their Andalusian heritage at last, and are dancing to some universal beat of the discos.

The middle classes of Spain are growing in numbers, wealth, and aspiration. In many a Spanish service station the ladies' lavatory is represented by an exquisite elbow-length glove and a rose, and the men's by an impeccable topper and a silver-headed cane – and somehow

The beach,
Benidorm

these old images, with their inferences of Noël Coward and the Astaires, properly represent the awakening of the Spanish bourgeoisie. They are in a familiar stage of sophistication. They have Popsy Krisps for breakfast, even if the packets do still find it necessary to assure the customer that no cooking is required. They wash their cars on Sunday afternoons. Their shops are full of washing machines, their roofs are cluttered with television aerials, and if they dine out they sometimes take their transistors along too, and prop them against the wine bottle. They are still thin on the ground, to be sure – they are almost entirely urban, and are still most numerous in the Basque and Catalan provinces. Every Spanish city, though, now has its quota, and one of these days we may expect the Spanish Babbitt, with his well-pressed suit and his prospects, once and for all to replace the cloaked and noble countryman as emblematic of his people.

Manners maketh man, perhaps, but history maketh manners. Already, as pastoral Spain retreats before the assaults of our material civilization, you may see the corrosion setting in. Hideous, vulgar, and gimcrack are the new tourist towns of Andalusia, where Spanish speculators have allied themselves with hordes of shady foreigners to develop the Costa del Sol; forgotten are the old instincts of form and balance, the organic strength of Spanish architecture, the sense of frank and decorous resignation. All is flash and easy profit. The truck-drivers of Spain are among the best in Europe, bringing to their calling the old courtesy and good sense of the muleteers; but the limousines of the new rich are driven with a rudeness, an ostentation, and an incompetence scarcely to be equalled anywhere.

So times change. The Spaniard, so grave, so courteous, so passionate, so reserved, turns out to be, when given the opportunity, much like the rest of us. He will push you in the supermarket, toot his horn at the traffic lights, leave the curtains open to impress the neighbours; for he is coming to terms with the world at last, and the world is teaching him how.

In the end it is bound to make the Spaniards more ordinary, as the petty squalors of industrial life overcome them too, and they lose their sense of separateness. It may be foolish to be proud and insular, but at least it makes for style. It may be wrong, even wicked, to remain a poor anachronism among the nations, but at least it kept Spain on a plane all her own, possessing what the theatre calls 'star quality', as distinct from the Swedens and the Switzerlands as a phoenix from a

Peñíscola

pair of pigeons. Progress is sure to weaken the Spanish identity, that powerful and often baffling abstraction, and the journey over Ronces-valles will inevitably lose some of its drama. Perhaps the ordinary Spaniards, often poor, often hungry, often bullied, often cold, will profit in the end; but the world, to whom the Spanish style stands as a reassurance of individual worth, come triumph come tragedy, come democracy or dictator – the world can only lose, as Spain becomes less Spanish, and the last illusions fade. 'Spain is an absurd country,' wrote Ganivet, 'and metaphysically impossible; absurdity is her nerve and mainstay. Her turn to prudence will denote the end.'

For though every country has its Sanchos, Quixote could only be Spanish, and often his illusions went deeper than the truth. To the squire it was only a brass bowl that they stole from the barber, but the knight looked beyond, and saw it to be the helmet of Mambrino the enchanter. 'Do you know what I think, Sancho? This famous piece, this enchanted helmet, must have fallen by some strange accident into the hands of someone who did not esteem it at its true value. So, not knowing what he was doing, and seeing that it was pure gold, he must have melted down the other half for the sake of the metal, and made from this half what looks like a barber's basin.'

ENVOI:
STATE
OF BEING

It is the beginning of an era in Spain, but more pertinently, it is the end of another. Nobody knows whether democracy will last in Spain, but it is historically certain that the despotism that died with General Franco was not a Spanish aberration, but was the Spanish political norm. It was one of the classic eras of Spanish history, for better or for worse, in which a despot supported by Church and Army strengthened the unifying forces of Spain, and clamped the country in a vice of conformity. If it saved Spain from the ravages of the Second World War, for years it set her apart too from the hopes and achievements of the peace – rather as the despotism of Philip II, long before, made Spain the greatest of the Powers, but condemned her to self-illusion.

Like Philip's, Franco's autarchy was shrouded in religiosity – not Christianity alone, but also a sort of dim Wagnerian vision of hero-gods and Valhallas, a gloomy level of devotion on which paganism, Catholicism and the apotheosis of the State could conveniently be mingled. They may scoff at it now, but vast numbers of Spaniards, I do not doubt, would still respond to this heady stimulant, if they were given the chance again. They love to think of themselves as incorrigible individualists, and if you believed their more starry-eyed apologists you would think them constitutionally incapable of suffering despotism. Such is not the case. More than most people, they seem to need a strong leader, and more than most they vibrate to the mass emotion and the communal life. They are easy to bully, as any petty bureaucrat

Valle de los Caidos

194

will demonstrate, as he harangues the submissive queue before his desk. They do not often defy the majority. Watch the Spaniards at a bull-fight, and you will see that when a matador succeeds, a frightening tide of hero-worship sweeps instantly around the crowd, and that when one fails, then the catcalls and whistles echo across the city, the insults are chanted like incantations, and not a single dissenting tremor of sympathy breaks the unison – the women stare pitilessly at that handsome failure, and even the matador's own assistants, standing there all gaudy behind the barricades, avoid his eye as he leaps lithe but crest-fallen out of the sand.

The Spaniards are negative individualists – there is nothing very constructive to their jealous egotism. Their social conscience is generally rudimentary, they are factional and often violent. They do have, to be sure, a healthy disbelief in the innate superiority of anybody to anybody else – 'as noble as the king, but not as rich', is the Castilian's traditional description of himself, and the Aragonese nobles used to swear loyalty to their king in the following stout formula: 'We who are as good as you swear to you who are no better than we, to accept you as our sovereign lord, provided you observe all our statutes and laws: *si no, no* – if not, not.' Goya once threw a plaster cast at the Duke of Wellington, and the Kings of Spain themselves, perhaps conscious that their autocracy must be impersonal to succeed, never signed their names to a document, only the words '*Yo, el rey* – I, the King'.

But once disciplined by the will of the majority, or by the inflexible command of Government, the Spanish people seem almost ideal material for dictatorship – strong, diligent, courageous, proud, patriotic, obedient, unimaginative. Autocracy is an old habit in Spain, and in Franco's day most Spaniards fell easily enough into its rhythms; life in his republic often looked like a sequence from some totalitarian propaganda film, as the jolly workmen bounced gregariously to work in the backs of lorries, as the pretty girls in kerchiefs sang songs and waved in potato fields, as the sailors marched along the Majorca waterfront singing patriotic songs, and the schoolchildren sat attentive and respectful beneath the Generalissimo's paternal portrait. On the other hand democracy, when they tried it between the wars, was an unsuccessful innovation, so unpractised were the people in its techniques, and so violent were the passions that its milder authority released.

Will it work better this time? It is true that Spain always seems to be yearning for some moment of fulfilment, some chance to flower, that nowadays only democracy can allow: but though the Spaniards are eagerly seizing their new opportunities, and political liberty is all the rage, somehow democracy does not yet feel natural to the place. It will take time, in a country where autocracy has so long seemed the natural order of things – organic, hereditary, bred in the bones, as much a part of the Spanish climate as the dead heat of the Castilian summer, or that knife-edge wind beneath the ribs.

The Spanish language has two words for the verb 'to be'. One is *estar*, which means to be in a particular condition, as a book is on a table, or your mother-in-law is ill. The other is *ser*, which means to be in a state of being, as grass is green and God's in his Heaven. The *estar* of Spain is shifting today, with its new veneer of modernism, but beneath it all the essential *ser* remains. Our graph ends with King Juan Carlos. We can be sure of nothing further. Perhaps ours is the last generation to glimpse Spain as the world has so long known her; or perhaps our children too, as they wander this enigmatic State, will recognize it still as Philip's disillusioned kingdom.

Some thirty miles north-west of Madrid a vast granite cross, the largest emblem of the Christian faith ever erected on earth, stands tremendously upon a ridge, visible almost from the capital itself, and surveying one of the most dismal battlefields of the Civil War. General Franco put it there, and inside the hill on which it stands he has tunnelled a vast granite crypt, longer than the nave of St. Peter's in Rome, and sumptuously decorated with statuary, tapestries, and bronze. Ostensibly this mausoleum is a memorial to all those, from either

Las Ramblas, Barcelona

side, who fell in the Civil War. Actually it is a monument to Spain herself, the *ser* of this country, the denuded soil and the empty plateau, the snow on the mountains, the heat and the cold and the poverty, the ever-present abstractions of God, death and Inquisition.

Seven hundred men worked every day for ten years to dig this place, and many of them were political prisoners of the regime. Franco lies now in a tomb before the high altar, and all day long the monks, the nuns and the soldiers file through, the tourists whisper awestruck, and the elaborately uniformed attendants, like cinema ushers, stand with their white-gloved hands reverently behind their backs. Sometimes an organ thunders through the chapels in a constant fortissimo, playing pompous hymns and marches. A frightening air of tomb or prison haunts the vault, the music deadens the senses, and all seems swollen, tragic and endless.

A mile or two along the ridge stands the Escorial, and the Vale of the Fallen is another door to the *coro* of Spain. From the road that runs between them you may look out across the desolate expanse of the *meseta*, and see Spain lying there below – 'a cloud of dust, left in the air when a great people went galloping down the highroad of history'. There it all is, like a mirage in the morning: the space and the dust and the pride of it all, the chuffing steam trains on the high plateau, the tall golden towers beside the rivers of Spain, the storks, and the priests, and the policemen. It is the kind of high prospect that hermits look for, when they want to sit down with a skull on the table, and think about the future.

INDEX
OF
HISTORICAL
EVENTS

B.C.

Under Phoenician, Greek, Cartha-
ginian, and Roman influence,
Spain emerged from dim barba-
rism to the most advanced of the
Roman subject provinces.

11th century B.C. Phoenicians
establish trading centres.
6th century B.C. Greeks establish
colonies.
218 B.C. Second Punic War begins
Roman conquest of Spain.

A.D.

The Visigothic kings, succeeding
to the order of Rome, ruled Spain
as a Christian nation for three centuries, with their capital at Toledo.

409 A.D. Vandals and other barbarians invade Spain from the
north.
414 Visigoths enter Spain, and
presently become her rulers.
589 Roman Catholicism adopted
as State religion of Spain.

The Moors captured most of Spain
in two years, but for the next seven
centuries engaged in desultory war
against the surviving Christian
kingdoms of the north, which
gradually fought their way southwards in the campaign of the
Reconquest.

711 Muslims invade Spain.
718 Battle of Covadonga, won by
surviving Christians of north.
756 Establishment of Córdoba
Caliphate.
1085 Toledo recaptured by Christians.

The end of the fifteenth century
brought Spain her most spectacular moment of success. United at
last under the Catholic Monarchs,
she expelled the last of the Moors,
sent her explorers to the New
World, and re-organized her society as the champion of Catholic
purity.

1479 Castile and Aragón united
under Isabel and Ferdinand.
1480 Introduction of Inquisition.
1492 Fall of Granada.
Columbus sails for America.
Expulsion of Jews.

The accession of the Hapsburgs to the Spanish thrones, together with the activities of the conquistadores in America, made Spain for a brief period the greatest power on earth.

The ignominious defeat of the Armada shattered Spain's confidence in herself, and during the next four centuries her story is one of decline: the loss of her empire, a succession of sterile wars in Europe, perpetual controversies about the succession, led at last to the ultimate catastrophe of the Spanish Civil War.

For nearly forty years Spain, half numbed still by the aftermath of the Civil War, moved tentatively, under the dictatorship of Francisco Franco, towards the end of isolation and the triumph of cosmopolitan, materialist values over her old insular traditions.

With the end of Franco's regime, the floodgates of democracy were opened and change rushed in, leaving Spain in a condition of excited but possibly perilous uncertainty.

1516 Charles I, the Holy Roman Emperor Charles V, succeeds to throne.
1519 Cortés lands in Mexico.
1532 Pizarro lands in Peru.
1556 Philip II succeeds to throne.

1588 Defeat of the Armada.
1609 Expulsion of the Moriscos.
1700 War of the Spanish Succession brings Bourbons to the throne.
1808 French occupation of Spain.
1811 Venezuela declares independence followed by other South American republics.
1833 First Carlist War.
1874 Second Carlist War.
1898 Spanish-American War.
1931 Republic proclaimed.
1936 Spanish Civil War.

1938 General Franco becomes head of Nationalist Government.
1939 Nationalist victory in Civil War.
1953 Treaty with the United States.
1955 Spain admitted to United Nations.

1975 Franco dies, Juan Carlos becomes King, and a democratic State is established.

INDEX

ACKNOWLEDGEMENTS

The publishers would like to thank the following for
permission to reproduce details from paintings in this book:

page 34:
Valentin de Zubiaurre: "The village authorities"
(MAS)/Madrid, Museo de Arte Contemporaneo

page 50:
Ramon de Zubiaurre: "Basque Sailor"
(MAS)

page 63:
Joaquin Sorolla y Bastida: "Fishermen from Valencia, 1903"
(Fine Art Photographs)

page 80:
John Phillip: "A Spanish Flower Seller, 1851"
(Fine Art Photographs)

page 91:
Richard Ansdell: "The Fair at Seville"
(Fine Art Photographs)

page 108:
Joaquin Sorolla y Bastida: "The Dance, Seville"
(Hispanic Society of America)

page 127:
Ramon de Zubiaurre: "Festival in a Basque Village"
(MAS/Bilbao, Banco Urquijo)

page 138:
Filippo Baratti: "A Market Town in Spain"
(Fine Art Photographs)

page 151:
Robert Kemm: "The Wedding of a Matador"
(Fine Art Photographs)

page 179:
Jose-Jimanes Aranda: "Washerwomen Disputing"
(Bridgeman Art Library/Victoria & Albert Museum)

Picture research by Jenny de Gex